THE FLU SEASON

AND OTHER PLAYS

THE FLU SEASON

AND OTHER PLAYS

WILL ENO

THEATRE COMMUNICATIONS GROUP
NEW YORK
2008

The Flu Season and Other Plays is published by Theatre Communications Group, Inc., 520 Eighth Avenue, 24th Floor, New York, NY 10018-4156

The Flu Season, Intermission and *Tragedy: a tragedy* are published by arrangement of Oberon Books Ltd., 521 Caledonian Road, Islington, London N7 9RH, UK.

This publication is made possible in part with public funds from the New York State Council on the Arts, a State Agency.

TCG books are exclusively distributed to the book trade by Consortium Book Sales and Distribution.

LIBRARY OF CONGRESS CATALOGING-IN-PUBLICATION DATA

Eno, Will, 1965–
The flu season and other plays / Will Eno.—1st ed.
p. cm.
ISBN 978-1-55936-291-7
I. Eno, Will, 1965– Tragedy. II. Eno, Will, 1965– Intermission. III. Title.
PS3555.N652F68 2007
812'.54–dc22   2007034925

Book design and composition by Lisa Govan
Cover design by John Gall
Cover photo by Caitlin Krol
Author photo by G. Lish/massmindwerks

First Edition, May 2008

For Gordon, and Gordon knows why,
and Emily, who was a great great friend,
and for Shevaun Mizrahi, indefinitely.

CONTENTS

THE FLU SEASON

Production History

The Flu Season was first produced on April 7, 2003, by the Gate Theatre in London. The director was Erica Whyman, the designer was Soutra Gilmour, the lighting designer was Anthony Simpson and the sound designer was Michael Oliva. The cast was:

PROLOGUE	Martin Parr
EPILOGUE	Alan Cox
MAN	Matthew Delamere
WOMAN	Raquel Cassidy
DOCTOR	Damien Thomas
NURSE	Pamela Miles

Dramatis Personae

PROLOGUE	A narrator, male (see Production Notes following the play)
EPILOGUE	A narrator, male (see Production Notes following the play)
MAN	Intelligent, somewhat scrappy, late twenties or so
WOMAN	Intelligent, somewhat delicate, late twenties or so
DOCTOR	Male, doctoral, dignified though somewhat distracted, fifties or so
NURSE	Female, maternal, also dignified though somewhat distracted, early fifties or so

Setting

The play takes place in a mental health institution of a not very specific type. (Though not specific, it is very certainly not meant to be any kind of shocking or cruel environment. *The Flu Season* is not in any way a critique of the mental health industry or of psychoanalysis. It is a play about the difficulty of love, the difficulty of being human, of making art.) The play also takes place in a theater, as each narrator makes clear.

We tell our little story, staring out. We come up with a beginning while knowing the end, and this is trouble. We trudge on, into winter, losing ground, looking back, trying, slipping, telling a tale of summer, a sinking feeling amid the leaving geese and slush. It's coming, little one. Truth. Real cold. Now, where's my shoes?

—FROM THE FILM
BY DINT OF THE BRIDGE'S COLLAPSE

PROLOGUE *(Enters, in darkness. Footsteps. Pause)*: Darkness and footsteps. A little pause. *(Pause)* It's quiet and dark. But you knew that. *(Pause)* I could leave it at that. I could leave it all alone, leave us all uncomforted by the shaky fiction of anything shared, of any common story. Let us wreck ourselves in the dark, shiver closer to death, slowly, unnoticeably, instead of making such a big production out of it. But I won't. So, savor it, the dark. Like everything, it's ending. Yes, as for the darkness, at least: The End. *(Lights up)* Hello. My name is Prologue. Welcome to a play whose title is *The Snow Romance*. It is a chronicle of love and no love, of interiors and exteriors, of weather, change, entry-level psychology, and time; but, oh, lo—what chronicle isn't. Composed one spring, it follows the lives of four or five people living in the season just previous. I'll be brief. We are in a sort of hospital. The time is almost winter. The lights fall.

(The lights don't fall.)

EPILOGUE: Right. *(Brief pause)* A couple quick things. About the title, the play is now called *The Flu Season.* A lot of downtime has gone by since the first draft was written, or, quote, composed. The new title stands for the fatigue, for all the sick days, the sick years, wasted in coming up with a title at all. *The Flu Season.* I don't know. Could use some work, another year of scribbling, erasing. There's always a different word, some other title, something better the language might cough up. My character, we'll call him "Epilogue." Could have also been called "Regrets." Or, "Mr. Sorry-So-Sorry." Could have been called, I don't know, "Steve Stevenson"—the names don't matter. Can you hear me okay? Can you see me? *(Motioning to the Prologue)* He can't. Strange. Theater. This. Certain things we have to live with. Little rules and lies. Anyway, I come later, after, a little more, maybe, coldly. I'll revise a line, add an afterthought, subtract a feeling. I'll try to speak plainly. But I liked that last part. It describes life. I quote: "I'll be brief. We are in a sort of hospital. The time is almost winter. The lights fall."

(The lights fall on the Prologue and Epilogue.)

ACT ONE

SCENE 1

The Man is sitting downstage, in very low light. The second half of the scene will take place on the other side of the stage, and the Woman and the Nurse can be seated there, now, in darkness, while the first half of the scene is played.

DOCTOR *(Enters upstage, near a door)*: All alone in the all-dark, are we? Sitting in the twilight of the exit light, dreaming of some great difference, some healing hand, some heavenly or electrical light? Or just sitting there? Which? There's a difference. Tell us. The shuffling coughing world awaits. Give us a little of your disquiet.

MAN: I'm not doing anything.

DOCTOR: Well, not anything or not, we still need the light. *(He turns on a light switch. Lights up)* It adds a sort of decorum to our proceedings, brightens up the otherwise muted decor of our shadowy procession. And it helps us see. But how was it, without it?

MAN: Darker.

DOCTOR: I see. Less light. But what about you? How are you?

MAN: No.

DOCTOR: I'm sorry? I said, "How are you?"

MAN: I'm sorry, I thought you said, "Who are you?"

DOCTOR *(Brief pause)*: Even if I had, wouldn't "No" still have been the wrong answer?

MAN: The mind doesn't work this way.

DOCTOR: What way?

MAN: Responsively. I don't know. Responsively.

DOCTOR: I'm sorry?

MAN: Nothing. Can I go lie down?

DOCTOR: First, I have to quickly ask you a question or two.

MAN *(Takes a very large breath in and holds his breath. He speaks with great difficulty)*: Yur tha dogdor. You know bess.

DOCTOR: The first question is, *(He reads)* "In your personal dealings with people, with the certain persons who people your immediate surroundings, have you ever personally felt it humanly necessary to present, solely for the sole and lone purpose of individuality itself, a persona, such that . . ."

(The Man is still holding his breath.)

This is not that important. Would you like to go lie down?

MAN *(Huge exhalation)*: I really would.

DOCTOR: We can talk later. I do need you to sign something. Nothing very serious or breathtaking, just some more paper for the future to shred. A form. Strictly a formality. *(He begins to fill out a form)*

MAN *(Watching the Doctor from across the desk)*: How do you do that?

8

DOCTOR: Do what?

MAN: Write upside down like that?

DOCTOR *(Flips the paper around, showing that he was writing right side up)*: Voilà!

MAN: Oh, right. I get so used to seeing things from my own perspective.

DOCTOR: I see. From my own, I guess, yes? Please sign.

MAN *(He signs)*: Voilà. *(Looking at his signature)* Look at that. It really is strictly a formality. This is me—strictly, formally me—but it's not the only me. There's a hundred ways I could do it, all different, all mine. Looking at my little slanted mess of a signature, I have to wonder where my life will take me.

DOCTOR: I'll show you your room.

MAN *(Looking back down at his signature)*: I should have seen that somehow.

(The Doctor and Man exit. Lights up. The Nurse is at a desk, the Woman seated before it.)

NURSE: I think that would be fine.

WOMAN *(Pause)*: What would? No one said anything. You're just going to start talking to me, totally out of the blue?

NURSE: I am. That's just how life goes. Maybe you've seen a baby born, or a grown-up die. Amazing. Totally out of the blue. And, as someone once said to someone, everything has to start somewhere.

WOMAN: Well, so, then, start.

NURSE: In fact, dear, we're almost finished. So, lastly, any allergy or injury or personal personal history that you would like to make public? Any distinguishing marks, inside or out? A birthmark in the shape of anything? Some internalized agony wholly without form? Any even sketchy sense of your character to help us empathize with you, to help us live more empathically, more heroically, within the life-size form of our own familiar pain?

WOMAN: No.

NURSE: Splendid. I will duly note that. *(She writes for ten or fifteen seconds in her notebook)*

WOMAN: Are they still spelling, "No," with just two letters, or is it more, now?

NURSE: Oh, this—I'm sorry. I'm just scribbling. You're probably wondering where my little scribbles will take you. Yes? Either way, it all comes to something. A period, at least. A comma, or, dot-dot-dot, in some sad cases. *(Pause)* Well, I think you'll be a wonderful—

WOMAN *(Interrupting)*: No, I won't. I won't be a wonderful anything. Whatever noun was about to come out of you. I'll be here until I leave here, and I was only here because some family—reportedly mine—brought me here, and left me here.

NURSE: Families are only groups of people. And groups of people mean well, they try. Unless they're angry mobs waving broken bottles and golf clubs, and even then, they still—in their way—try. Here, we also try to create a familial atmosphere. Or at least we try to act like a group of people. And the grounds are beautiful, this lovely time of year. The temperature dropping. Fall. Us, trying. The wonderful maple trees.

WOMAN: Yes, wonderful wonderful. Beautiful trees shedding their leaves, as I disintegrate into an animal, snow gently falling onto the uncombed hair of me, a cold cold girl, a sometime bitch in heat.

NURSE: Yes, well, you're tired, I'm sure, and possibly a little more elegiac than the situation seems to call for. I'll show you where your room is.

(They exit.)

PROLOGUE: In the world of our world, it is now late afternoon, a few days later. Our new admissions are settling in. The setting autumn sun is streaming through the thinning trees on the hospital property's edge, setting a kind of mood in the world. We are in the Crossroads Psychiatric Retreat Center. We are at a pay phone in the hall.

EPILOGUE: No argument here. It's getting darker, trees are dying. A few days later, a pay phone in the hall.

Scene 2

The Man is standing near a pay phone. The Woman enters.

WOMAN: I need to call somebody.

MAN: I'm waiting for someone to call.

WOMAN: I'll only be a second.

MAN: What if you suddenly find something else to talk about?

WOMAN: What if your phone call never comes?

MAN: What if the place you call is filled with people you haven't talked to in years? A line of loved ones and distant cousins, lined up through the house, waiting for their chance to get on the phone and twirl their hair and talk to you?

WOMAN: What if the person you're saying is going to call wrote the number down wrong and then lost the tiny piece of paper and was lying in the first place when he said he'd call at all?

MAN: It's a she. And she'll call. Go make your second-long call somewhere else. This is for normal human use. Phone calls lasting into the minutes and hours, years of long-distance and polite chatter, trailing off into raging and expensive silences. Humanity, on the horn. Conversation.

WOMAN: Fine. So make some conversation.

MAN: I will. *(Pause)* Nice weather I'm having. Yes, I would have to agree with myself, there. That's a nice haircut I have. Yes, thank you, it is but a sign of human civilization. Like standing up straight and not eating worms, it's not something I can really take credit for. *(The Woman begins to walk away)* And I see you wander through life in a social architecture called the family, the rubbley remains of which we build our new relations on. Yes, we do, and we use the same name and share the same features and we all move apart so as to later hold reunions. *(The Woman is gone)* Ice cream, you scream. This is how the mind works. Poorly. Around. On the ruin of the last thought. I'm glad we had this little chat. Et cetera. "Social architecture." I'm an idiot. She has nice hair. A last ruined thought.

PROLOGUE: He is certainly outgoing and verbal, certainly expectant and full of hope, standing by a phone that doesn't take incoming calls. She is walking back and forth somewhere, ingoing, unverbal, biting her nails, rethinking things, rethinking her life. But cut to the offices of the doctor and the nurse! It is morning, days later.

EPILOGUE: In a little while, we begin to depart from an earlier reality, from the original little mess of real life we built our play on. Hardly even noticeable. All the sweat and pain. All the lying and pretending, the rethinking, the revising into ruin. A signature move. It's only natural. If we could control life, it wouldn't be life. If we could control our likeness of it, it wouldn't be a likeness.

SCENE 3

The Nurse is in a chair, the Woman on a couch. On the other side of the stage, in very separate light, the Doctor is in his chair, with the Man on a couch.

WOMAN: He stayed waiting, I left. That's the story. I don't know. *(Pause)* Can I leave?

NURSE: In a little. Once—I'm reminded—I didn't know, either. On a train, in a dress, in the winter. Me, and the snow coming down into the ocean that the tracks ran along, as if in some famous short story. I saw a horse, from the train. I was on my youthful way south to see if someone might marry me, a man I had already given my hand and the rest of my body to, because that's what you did when you did that in those days. Only a pony really. Are you cold? He said no, go home—essentially, get lost. That horse looked cold, standing in the middle of such a snowy and fictional-seeming winter. Or, pony. All the frozen marsh water around her. I never understood. The tall dead grasses. I assume it was a female. I was pretty. Not as pretty as you. Pretty enough, I thought, but, maybe not. What changed, I wanted to ask him. Cute, I guess you would say. No. Pretty, I was pretty when I was young. The way you are. The way you—I mean this as a compliment—will have been. Nice horsie, pretty girl.

WOMAN: Thank you. I'm sorry, can I go?

NURSE: No, dear. What I learned from all this is that I didn't learn that much. Live and learn—but not that much. *(Pause)* We still have some time.

DOCTOR: How goes life here, too fast, too slow? Happily, lamentably, timelessly, around, not at all, so many choices—how goes it?

MAN: I saw someone, the other day. I tried to make conversation.

DOCTOR: Really? Because, I saw someone, once. Once, I, yes, standing ankles-deep in a brook watching geese flying by, saw someone, once. I was thinking of the shape of a horse and trying to picture the cloud that might best represent it. Who comes along but—life is too remarkable—a woman. She was so pretty-looking, her collarbones, or, you know, clavicle, her clavicles, and so on, down the bones of her body. I climbed out of my water, crying hello, crying hi. I proposed all sorts of things to her. She slowly declined, over the coming months. I invited her to the ocean. She said no and no and never and then, one coming month, yes. We were together for a time. She threw me a surprise party. I had a mild stroke. Everyone came. She gave me an antique train set and I was rushed to the hospital. Some people knock looking backward as a way to live. I do not. Never did.

NURSE: I've felt a lot. As many people have. Where I distinguish myself is, I stand outside at night. I try to make new constellations out of the old stars, if there are any old stars out. Sometimes it rains. Or there's sleet, or nothing. I don't know if this distinguishes myself. I remember I was so hurt. I stand there. Or I don't. Is this a lonely picture? I'm a professional. This may all seem as if it's . . . I don't know. But it isn't. Unless it is. And if so, then, there you go. But all you need to know is that I, like the rest, like you, sit here with a serious history, with little and real fears and dreams, a heart and two eyes, looking out, from a body of bones, watching you and the rest of the world for some sign. I'm looking at you. Hello. *(Brief pause)* We have a little more time.

DOCTOR: I loved her and felt ugly. I grew to hate the way I walked, my stupid posture. I saw my dull reflection glaring at me from windows and mirrors, saying to me, "What are you looking at?" I asked myself, "Am I beautiful, inside?" No response, inside, except gurgling. None, without, except a different gurgling. People died. Winter and Summer Olympics passed. I slowly declined. I used to love the Butterfly, in swimming. The Downhill, in skiing. You probably don't see me as a man who loved so much. I, like everyone, was and was so for very long. Summer or winter, I cheered for everyone. I learned the stories of our nation's young athletes, their role models, subjects they failed in school, how hard they worked, and in such awful weather. I loved a lot. Instead of her. I don't know why.

NURSE: My one true love: a meaningless fling. I looked for the horse on the ride home.

DOCTOR: It wouldn't have killed me if things had been different.

MAN: My life is going to be different.

WOMAN: My life story unfurls itself before me in gleaming ripples and hopeful waves of never-ending and over-written difference.

NURSE (*Earnestly*): Good for you. Really, darling. (*Pause*) I'm surprised, as I get older and people look me less and less in the eye, how nothing ever changes. It seems that the way things seem is the way they're going to stay seeming. There's that old saying: "Buck teeth are buck teeth." And that other old saying: "Horses always smell like horses."

WOMAN: Are those really old sayings?

NURSE: They will be, someday, if people start saying them now. (*She looks at her watch*) Speaking of someday, we don't have any more time, for today.

MAN: You know what's probably pretty interesting, is that I don't think I've ever really—

DOCTOR (*Interrupting. He is making notes. His pen appears to have run out of ink. He shakes it, vigorously*): Hang on a sec. (*He finds another pen, has to draw scribbles with it for a moment, in order for the ink to begin running)* There we go. *(Shaking his head, smiling)* Ink.

(The scene ends.)

PROLOGUE: It's evening. The cold air, dark sky, and historical stars. Faraway traffic goes unhonkingly by, with daylight savings over, the beaches uncrowded. It's past twilight. Geese are flying noisily overhead, mated for life, as the duck-hunting season opens. Houses and corporate headquarters are festively decorated, empty except for the light. 'Tis the season hardest to suffer, and better to hibernate through. So now we, to the TV room, for some television.

EPILOGUE: Winter isn't sad. You've had happy times in winter. And sad ones in summer. Life goes by year-round. People get married in sleet storms. People get cancer on soft summer evenings, sitting by the radio, looking up words in a dictionary. The wonderful world falls apart around the clock. You know this from experience, if you've ever had any. And there's nothing necessarily sad about anything. Or happy. I just wanted to make that clear. Am I making myself clear? It doesn't matter. You don't care. You're thinking about yourself. Our scene moves to the TV room.

SCENE 4

The Woman turns on the television. The television faces upstage.

TELEVISION: . . . cars with their lights on coming down Main Street, through this once darkened little town, now alight with grief. All, in a state of shock at the loss—the drowning—of the popular Williams family. The area always has a tragedy to grieve, but rarely a one as grievous as this. A family, in whole, pulled drowned from the local pond, after an evening of skating, a winter's outing undertaken too early in the season. We are all on thin ice, but, for some of us, it's even thinner. Young and old, they still wore their skates, tightly tied on to make up for their weak ankles. Whatever they wore, all those generations now are now gone; and, though this reporter understands that this would have naturally happened eventually, this reporter also understands it is tragic it happened now. One bright spot, they leave no family behind. They are survived by only their neighborhood and house. No legal battles will ensue. It's all settled. They're dead. Live, I am in Carlisle. Stay tuned for some holiday gift ideas and tips on ways to keep your car battery from freezing. Reporting for channel—

(The Woman turns off the television. Pause. The Man enters.)

MAN: Hi.

WOMAN: Well, if it isn't you.

MAN: Yup. Or, would it be, "Nope." Hi.

WOMAN: Did your phone call come?

MAN: That thing doesn't take incoming phone calls, it turns out. Did you find somewhere to make yours from?

WOMAN: I decided not to call.

MAN: I feel bad.

WOMAN: It isn't your fault. It was better I didn't call. I'm glad.

MAN: Oh good. I'm glad. I still feel bad. *(Pause)* Not because of anything to do with you.

WOMAN: I'm sorry.

MAN: It isn't your fault. As I think I just, you know, I don't know, I think, pretty clearly, said. Do you have change for the laundry room?

WOMAN: I might. *(She begins to look for change)* Did you watch the sun go down tonight?

MAN *(Pause)*: Don't you see what's happening here?

WOMAN: No.

MAN: Me neither.

WOMAN: Did you see the sunset?

MAN: Oh, right—the sun, going down. No. I didn't. I think I can honestly say, I did not.

WOMAN: You should have. It was pretty. It was cold-looking. A person could come up with all kinds of words, if he sat down and tried.

MAN: I'm sure. *(Pause)* Bye. *(Begins to leave)*

WOMAN: Do you have anyone come, for visiting hours?

MAN: I'm separated.

WOMAN: Is your wife near here?

MAN: Oh I'm not married. I just kind of meant—

WOMAN *(Interrupting)*: Me neither.

MAN: I thought I would be divorced by now. Sometimes I see a rickety little house with broken shutters and a tiny swimming pool and I think, "I'd like to get married, and then get divorced, and then live there." But I never met the right person. See you around.

WOMAN: Didn't you need quarters?

MAN: No. No, thanks. That was just a need I had. Something to act on. And so I did. And here we are. Bye, again.

(He exits. The Woman exits.)

PROLOGUE: Do things seem aimless? Maybe that's how things are. Do you think anyone has a future? An aim? The man and woman? The nurse and doctor? Are you an optimist? Do you see a love scene on the sunless horizon? Are you good at making things up? And can you properly repress?

My questions won't get us anywhere. Nor will my answers. But, so, to the group therapy room, for group therapy, in the morning.

EPILOGUE: Is the main action of the play someone with a pencil in his hand, sitting at a desk in the morning, trying to come up with a word for sunset? Is the through-story (so-called) thrown away? As he tries to revise the play and create ornate metaphors for simple blunt facts? As the old fears creep in. The old story. Is repetition a failure in daring, or a step toward deliverance? Could be both. Don't know, never knew. So, to the group therapy room, for group therapy, in the morning. I quote. Or, repeat. Because, why wouldn't I? That's what we do.

SCENE 5

The Doctor, Nurse, Man and Woman are seated together.

DOCTOR: It was always one of the most beautiful places and times in the world for me.

NURSE *(Long pause)*: What was?

DOCTOR: Didn't I say? I'm sorry. The Netherlands, when I went when I was young. The days were beautiful girls. Blue skies, yellow flowers, the world's largest diamond. Decent drugs, Anne Frank's attic, tall blond Dutch women on vintage bicycles, and me. I saw the queen at a tennis game.

NURSE *(Pause)*: How does traveling make people feel?

WOMAN: I've never been anywhere. No, yes I have.

MAN: Sad.

NURSE: I'm sorry?

MAN: Traveling makes me feel sad.

NURSE: Why, do you think?

MAN: Why do I *think*? I guess because—

NURSE *(Interrupting)*: Why do you think it makes you feel sad?

MAN: I don't *think* it makes me feel sad. Traveling makes me feel sad. F E E L. S A D.

NURSE: Oh, a speller.

DOCTOR: Maybe—M A Y B E—it has something to do with all the things going past in the window. The sadness, I mean. Life life life, mile after mile. You're a smiling baby, a reckless teen, a tax-paying adult, a corpse. Bang bang bang. You're just getting the hang of the toilet and, suddenly, time to pick out a coffin. I'm kidding. Or, exaggerating. Slightly. *(Brief pause)* Amsterdam.

(Everyone looks at the Doctor. Pause.)

WOMAN: Once I lived a whole summer with a friend's family. I did everything they did. I got stung by bees and tried drinking and simple kinds of kissing. It was hard being away and then hard being home. Is that something like what you were looking for someone to say?

NURSE: Just like, dear. Thank you. I guess we're all away from somewhere. Away from some house on some street, or from some position in relation to the body of the mother. By dint of our being here. Did anyone know that "dintless" was a word?

MAN: Did anyone ever see a movie called *By Dint of the Bridge's Collapse*?

WOMAN: Is that where the shoeshine boy is always staring at the girl who sells flowers? But there's no reason to buy flowers and no one has good shoes because the whole town is poor and sad. He's a poet. Or he's thinking about it. The girl only eats vitamins.

DOCTOR: And she was played by Susette de Baronelle, who I was a little in love with. Still a little am.

NURSE: Movies are wonderful. I didn't see that particular one.

MAN: And his brother keeps bringing different animals home and naming them all the same thing. And, right, the main boy stares at the main girl. You never know if they ever meet, or ever fall in love. The town is in a sort of quarantine.

DOCTOR *(Looking at his watch and his notepad)*: I know this has only been a few pages, but we have to stop. *(He takes out an appointment book)* Sorry. Funny, life. We don't even have time to misrepresent ourselves. We hardly have time to make a tragic error of our lives. Oh, well; ah, well. Now, before everyone leaves, I need to change next week. *(He begins writing in the appointment book and, as he's writing, says, offhandedly)* I'm starting to think it was Belgium I went to, and that I only read about Amsterdam.

PROLOGUE: The weeks change anyway. Another little pause in the world. *(Pause. Perhaps the Prologue turns around to survey the quiet stage)* Then, right on cue, here comes more time, giving us life, rushing past, taking it away. Time. Do you feel it? Ladies and gentlemen, do you? It's there. I wouldn't know how it feels. In words. That's all right. It's late on an early winter's evening, and we, to the rec room, rush!

EPILOGUE: In other words: tick-tock, tick-tock. But, again, well enough said. "The weeks change anyway." Time is important here, to us. The general sweep of it, not its particularities. "Sweep" is the wrong word, but, you'll live with it. Gentle, deadly. Slow and violent, it just goes by. I wouldn't look for some life-changing event. Except life, or illness, or death. This is all supposed to be at least plausible, after all, our play. Real American realism. But, so, what changed your life? Forever. Whatever it was, it's probably still doing it. Tick-tock. Or to put it another way, at what moment did

your life suddenly stay the same forever. It's night in the
rec room. We claim. You're sitting there in the dark.
Strangers, forever, on either side of you.

SCENE 6

*The Man is assembling a balsa-wood toy airplane. The Woman
walks by in the background, upstage. She stops to look and listen,
unseen. Perhaps, it is in this moment that she begins to fall in love
with him.*

MAN: All quiet, as I assemble a balsa-wood toy airplane. I'll use
a rubber band to drive the propeller. Once finished, once
this project of mine is done, when the little toy can finally
fly, it won't help anything, but it will fly high above this
dirt-bound life, without changing anything, and then crash,
without end, until it's over.

(The Woman exits.)

PROLOGUE: Night's over. And it's morning. And we return to
rooms we thought we left. We return to the rec room. It
makes you wonder. Have life and the whole world already
been written—been foreseen, foretold, long been forborne?
Is the ending of the story already in your bones? The
fevered climax already long in your cold blood?
EPILOGUE: Maybe. Probably. But you hope that along the way
there will still be, sometimes, a surprise. We're back in the
rec room, yes. The woman enters, yelling:

SCENE 7

WOMAN: Surprise! *(She enters holding a lit birthday-cake candle. The balsa-wood airplane is completed. She sings)* "Happy birthday to you." *(She speaks)* You know the middle part. *(She sings the final line)* "Happy birthday to you." *(She speaks)* I guess you know the ending, too. The fevered climax is probably already long in your cold blood. But it seemed unkind somehow, or anti-art, not to sing it.

MAN: My birthday isn't until spring.

WOMAN: How would I know that? We've hardly talked. That's what makes this so gracious an act. So mysterious.

MAN: It is pretty gracious an act. Pretty mysterious. Thanks. *(He holds up the candle)* Was there a cake that came with this?

WOMAN: My uncle died on his birthday last year.

MAN: I'm sorry. He's in a better place, I guess.

WOMAN: We don't know. He had a nice house. He died.

MAN: I'm sorry.

WOMAN: It's not your fault. Is it? It isn't. His gravestone read, "Here lies the late myself, dead as far as the eye can see."

MAN: Cake? *(He feeds her an imaginary piece of cake)*

WOMAN: Mmmm. Not bad. Here, you. *(She feeds him a piece. Pause)* You put your hand in my mouth, just then.

MAN: Ditto you yours in mine.

WOMAN: What a cold and intriguing sentence. I remember, once, I don't know why—oh, I know why: because it was cold. And intriguing. To me. But, so, up north, once, I threw all this outdoor furniture off the roof of a museum. Chairs and tables and glass ashtrays. That was the start of my adulthood. I was trying to become a lifeguard. I was supposed to be rescuing things. Around that point, people stopped returning my calls, generally. I started acting really psychological. When I bled—you know, girl stuff—I bled too much.

MAN: Oh. A lot of that kind of went over my . . . so, did you ever become a lifeguard? Wasn't the water cold? I got really emotional next to a screen door, once. So there was that. *(Pause)* Have you seen outside? It looks like rain. Or snow.

WOMAN: What does?

MAN: It does, what else, the—I don't know—sky, the firmament. The, um, welkin. We pretended to eat pretend-cake. I find that sort of interesting. We shared something that doesn't—

WOMAN *(Interrupting)*: It was interesting. I'm looking forward to seeing you again.

MAN: Are you leaving?

WOMAN: No. It was for children, I should add.

MAN: What was? The museum was?

WOMAN: I should go.

MAN: Did I say something?

WOMAN: Did it sound to you as if you said something? I didn't hurt anyone, throwing the stuff off. Even though I broke everything. And could have killed someone. I feel as if I should go. And that usually means I should go. Bye. *(She exits)*

MAN: Bye. *(To himself)* I feel as if I should go.

(The scene ends.)

PROLOGUE: Despite winter coming at these two from every angle and direction, one can sense a little spring in their speech. Them two, warming toward each other. Our scene moves ahead one week. And it's snowed. And it's night. On the grounds, somebody built six snowmen, facing different ways, standing too close together. And our love story has progressed without us. Will we catch up to it, overtake it? Either way, to the sunroom, in the moonlight.

EPILOGUE: The birthday scene was a happy scene. But let's not be precious. It wasn't even anyone's birthday. And if not these two talking, then two others. Or one of them and someone else, some third person. The history of plays and the history of the world is a set of the same conversations being had by different people. We've all been through them. "You are the only one, forever," we swear, having sworn it twice, or more. People are liars, but, liars are people. Take me. I'm an excellent example. So, forgive and forget. Then die and be forgotten. Or, I don't know—maybe there's more to it. But in the meantime these two are becoming sort of lovely together. I admit. A handsome couple. Either way, we are in the sunroom. A week later, a night, the Winter Solstice.

Scene 8

The Nurse and Doctor are seated, wearing winter jackets. They hold ice skates. There is a bowl of plastic fruit on the table before them.

NURSE: They're probably having one of their very particular conversations, in which they both take such solace. I remember those conversations, those whispered times—so original, such pure meaning and total motivation, you know? You go ahead. I'll wait.

DOCTOR: No, no. I'll wait with you. It'll make the time go by faster.

(Long pause. The time doesn't go by faster. They fidget.)

I haven't been skating in years.

NURSE: How about that heartbreaking story of that family skating. And the ice broke and they all fell through? Williams, was it? The name?

DOCTOR: I think, yes. Imagine, a dead family. When they dragged the bodies out, the whole town could hardly keep staring. I thought I might speak about it, might try to bang it up into words, at the conference on the National Grief in the spring. To the which, by the way, I would, I must say, of course—it goes without saying—love you to come.

NURSE: Please, Doctor. Must you be so forward?

DOCTOR: I'm sorry, you're right. There was a lot of punctuation in that invitation. But it would be wonderful and helpful. Give it some thought. Period. Speeches about grief during the day, a whirlpool, a shower, and then cocktails at seven. It's in one of those little sea towns. We could take the train down.

NURSE: I haven't been to the ocean since I was a girl. I was a girl at one time, Doctor, as you are probably aware.

DOCTOR: We could play golf. Doctors are good at golf. Although I never played. Don't tell anyone, I could lose my license. And I was aware.

NURSE: I would love to see the sun set somewhere different.

DOCTOR: So it's decided. Is it decided? Well, you think, and then decide.

NURSE: I will.

DOCTOR *(Looking at the bowl of fruit)*: These are fake, I just noticed.

(The Man and Woman enter.)

NURSE: And here they are! Come on, you two. Everyone is waiting.

WOMAN: You go ahead. I'm cold. I want to put on more clothes.

DOCTOR: Okay, but quickly now. Time's a wasting. There's only so much cocoa. That's my philosophy.

NURSE: You can't go wrong with a philosophy like that. Also, "Don't get sick in Europe," someone once told me. *(To the Man)* You need a hat. And hurry. We're going to light some sparklers.

(The Nurse and Doctor exit.)

WOMAN: Let's stay. I've seen a sparkler before.

MAN: Okay. Are you thinking what I'm thinking?

WOMAN: Are you thinking about when I burned my hand one year on New Year's Eve?

MAN: No.

WOMAN: Then no.

MAN: You look pretty.

WOMAN: Maybe I am pretty.

MAN: That would explain it. *(Pause)* Where were you hiding yourself today?

WOMAN: In the basement, behind the hot-water heater, in fear.

MAN: You missed exercise this morning.

WOMAN: I said I was under the weather. And behind the hot-water heater. I always liked exercise.

MAN: I bet you throw like a girl.

WOMAN: I am a girl.

MAN: Oh, hi. *(Brief pause)* Are your mother and father still together?

WOMAN: My father is. *(Brief pause)* But don't change subjects so fast. Because, just don't, please. Swimming is an interest I have. Let's talk about that. "What Swimming Is Like." Begin. Discuss. Enlarge. You have an average lifetime.

MAN: Swimming is different. From walking.

WOMAN: I see.

MAN: It's fun.

WOMAN: I see. Go on.

MAN: I'll never be how you think.

WOMAN: Oh.

27

MAN: Whales swim.

WOMAN: They do. Every day of the week.

MAN: There's enough room in the ocean for everyone in the world to have room to drown in. Do you see? *(He looks at the ceiling, speaks quickly)* But don't leave me, don't leave me, *(She moves to his side)* please don't leave me, please—

WOMAN *(Interrupting. Puts her hand on his shoulder)*: Here I am, I'm right here—

MAN *(Interrupting. Unkindly. He shrugs her hand off)*: Listen, can't you see I'm in the middle of something?

NURSE *(Enters)*: I forgot my scarf. Come on, you two. Don't just sit around here and miss everything. Okay, Miss Everything? *(She playfully flicks the Woman with her scarf)* And Mister Everything Else. The world is racing by and Doctor is skating around backward. He also just proposed to me that we all build an igloo. Does my hair look okay? Do I look, would you say, crazed, at all? Anyway, hurry. *(She exits)*

MAN: I'm sorry I yelled.

WOMAN: You didn't yell. *(Pause)* I don't want to miss everything. I really don't. I like everything.

MAN: Me neither. *(Pause)* I meant to yell.

WOMAN *(Pause)*: Name a season.

MAN: Winter.

WOMAN: Name another.

MAN: Spring.

WOMAN: We were made for each other.

MAN: Name an animal.

WOMAN: The otter.

MAN: Name another.

WOMAN: No, thanks.

MAN: We were.

WOMAN: Can we go be alone somewhere?

MAN: Both of us?

WOMAN: Yeah.

MAN: I know just the place.

WOMAN: Where?

MAN: I don't know, I've just heard people say that before.

WOMAN: How about your room?

MAN: If you don't mind the state it's in.

WOMAN: No.

MAN: And you don't mind that it's mine.

WOMAN: No.

MAN: Or that everything in it is mine. If you don't mind that loss shall be yours. And then even that will be taken away. And it might be messy. Are you allergic to dust?

WOMAN: No.

MAN: I want you to have the last word.

WOMAN *(Pause)*: Sympathy?

(They exit, him carrying her.)

PROLOGUE: What more could anyone want? What would anyone add? And why? And how would he phrase it? *(Brief pause)* I'll say this. Their skin is young. And they know nothing. Unlike ourselves, whose skin is old and who know nothing. But onward. There's no need to show what we all can so easily imagine. For instance, her taking his hand in hers and running it over her mouth, wetting it, running it over each breast, to down between her legs where all of herself comes together. All in a single fluid movement. And then him responding in kind, whispering into her eye, gently pulling her hair. They both say, "God." They both come to an understanding. And it's over. They lie all over each other. *(Pause)* Now it's late. The skaters have all come in. What cocoa is left over is frozen. The doctor fell and sprained his ankle, having fun and showing off. Nobody drowned. Winter has officially begun. Somebody lost a mitten. It's quiet and nothing more need be said.

EPILOGUE: Probably not. Probably not. *(Pause)* But, feelings between the man and woman, yes. The two characters seem right, beside the other, like the characters of the bird and the rock in ancient Chinese writing, beside the other. One bird, one stone. What is between the man and the woman is starting to seem inevitable, as with the rock and the bird. Will they be beside themselves forever? Do you follow my drift? From away from where we were? Is it noticeable yet? For I have one, a drift. All will painfully make itself painfully clear. Oh, but for now, such splendor, the liquid movements, the responding in kind, the hair, the hands, my God. Almost makes you . . . *(He stares off, wistfully. Returns abruptly)* I don't know. The room of the man.

SCENE 9

MAN: Do you see children anywhere on your horizon? A little baby screaming out of you? A new father standing frozen in horror behind his rented video equipment, trying to smile and focus? And a new voice in the world, crying? A new cry. Is that so crazy-sounding?

WOMAN: No.

MAN: Once I was younger with legs unbroken and dreams undreamt, years before I'd met or left anyone, and I looked forward to the future, and my mouth on you, parting the ocean and your legs, baying at the moon and earth, crying, "Mother Mother," or "Not Mother, Not Mother," wanting only to be lonely and home, to be drenched on the inside with blood, as usual, waiting, a man in a house, all the lights out, this is my vision, et cetera, et cetera. *(Pause)* Is that so crazy-sounding?

WOMAN: A little. But I could see a child. We could take family trips to the beach. You'd look for a place for our towel. I'd do that thing, pull my suit down from where it had ridden up. We'd take showers under those little weak showers they have in front of the giant ocean. And get something to eat. Maybe I'd lower your fly while we're driving home. The baby, asleep. A wet road map. Showering at home. You have pretty bones in your face. I would always lose my keys. You could type upstairs. Is this too scattered-sounding?

MAN: No.

PROLOGUE: Ah, love.

WOMAN: You should have the last word.

(The Nurse and Doctor enter at the other side of the stage, but remain in a separate playing area from the Man and Woman.)

MAN: Sympathy is such a good one. But let's see. Ocean, no; medication, no; redemption, no; cocoa, no; myself, no; salvation, no; it isn't summer, trust, or honesty, no. It's from Latin I have a feeling. I don't know. "Dire"? Is "dire" Latin? Is "Latin" Latin?

(The Man and Woman exit.)

NURSE: I think it's beautiful.

DOCTOR: It's a little unheard of, isn't it? I never heard of anything like this. I fear for them.

NURSE: I'm sure they fear for themselves just fine.

DOCTOR: How far have things progressed? If I may use so clinical a term. See, there's the problem. This growing clinicality. The old heartbreaking songs don't break my heart any-more. I haven't cried for the last five Olympics. But, how far?

NURSE: Far, I'd imagine, from that distant look they give each other. Those old songs will break your heart again, or the new ones will, when they're old. *(Pause)* I saw people ice-fishing, driving in this morning. There was a little bird flying over all the holes. How is your ankle healing?

DOCTOR: Correctly, I think, I thank you. I'm glad it's not broken. You'd have to carry me all over that conference.

NURSE: Which I would do with a smile. A grimace, I guess. A sort of pained, burdened, hyperventilating but not unhappy grimace. A smile.

PROLOGUE: Outside the window, a kite in a tree is covered in ice. People's bodies looked changed in the distance of the parking lot—hunched, closed, as seen in ultrasound—as they struggle with their frozen car door locks. Something to behold. And how long can they be beheld? How long can an image be kept in mind? I wouldn't hold your breath. Go stretch. I need to relieve myself. We'll take a little break, an intermission. Please come back, and, if you do, maybe you'll find that the cushion of your seat is cold and has given up the shape that you gave it, that there is no trace of you but your absence and a few gum wrappers. No trace. Imagine that. Hard to conceive. Almost impossible for us to conceive. See you soon.

EPILOGUE *(Stands as if about to deliver a soliloquy, seeming to be considering many things)*: Fifteen minutes.

(Lights down.)

ACT TWO

SCENE 1

Lights up on the Man and Woman, seated next to each other, but not touching. They stay very still. Lights down. They exit.

PROLOGUE: You've come back. Some time passed, in the last few minutes. Christmas did. Life continued. Christmas ended. Those decorations that made it through the wind and cold unbroken now are all down and put away. Whatever was frozen, froze harder. On the south lawn are snow forts and snow angels losing their child-made form. Very very north of here, a polar bear is eating a seal cub. And far over that, a dead satellite launched from Florida, America, during an earlier presidency, is floating out of control in freezing outer space. Back on Earth, we are in the reading room, in the common era.

EPILOGUE: What if you were writing a play, or doing anything, and your feelings changed? You didn't even know how you felt anymore, or what you thought. You couldn't keep going. The image disintegrated. Your mind wasn't up to it, or your heart. Would your claim to realism be lost if you didn't somehow incorporate the change, the not-knowing, the cold feeling? Even if only subtly? Would you just abort the whole thing? Turn your back on everyone and wash your hands of the whole bloody mess? What would you do, back on Earth? If this were you? If this were yours? *(Pause)* We move our scene to the reading room, sure, why not, in the common era.

Scene 2

Lights up on the Man and Woman. He is reading.

WOMAN: Where were you yesterday?

MAN: I had to take some tests.

WOMAN: What kind of tests, blood tests? History tests?

MAN: I took a Spielberger Rage and Anger Index, a Van Beck Depression Composite, a Taylor Manifest Anxiety Scale, and, just out of curiosity, a Minnesota Multiphasic Personality Inventory.

WOMAN *(Pause)*: How did they go?

MAN: I think I did really well.

WOMAN *(Pause)*: What are you reading?

MAN: The dictionary.

WOMAN: How is it?

MAN: You know the joke. It's a little wordy. The verbs are good, at the beginning. You get sick of them.

WOMAN: I'll wait for the movie. *(Pause)* You don't think that's funny?

MAN: Listen to this. *(He reads)* "Hilaktia: Disorder named for Greek ruler whose vivid nightmares of winter caused him to die and his body to manifest all signs of having frozen, despite the season being summer, the weather being warm. He wrote several plays, which survive in fragments or not at all. The disorder is characterized by a flight of ideas, a fear of the mind, and disregard for language and others. Treatable, with bright light, photographs, medicative therapies."

WOMAN *(Pause)*: What am I supposed to think about that?

MAN: You got me. Something, though. You'd think you'd think something. *(Pause)* Don't you ever change clothes? I'm sorry I said that—you look fine. But don't you? Forget I said that. Forget I said I'm sick of you and your body and sick of our story. One side of me is like saying—I don't know. Forget it. Listen to me, my sucky vocabulary. Blah. Blahhh. I wonder if I have that General's disease. Or, whatever, "ruler."

WOMAN: Maybe you just need—

MAN *(Interrupting)*: Thanks, I'll try that.

PROLOGUE: Do you remember somebody mentioning an otter? When verb followed noun, when the man and woman spoke lovingly and plainly in simple yups and good old household nopes? The woman said—it was such a nice line—"Yes." I forget what the man had asked her. I forget the exact feeling. But I can use the word "beautiful." I could say that. I could say a lot of words, if I sat down and tried. And I do know where this is going. So, to someplace! Lights, action!

EPILOGUE: Darkness, inaction. As an aside, have you ever been stung by a bee that had nothing against you? Or bitten by a dog who otherwise seemed to like you? Or fell, due to a gravity not your own? Or hurt someone you loved, or used to love, or never did? Ever suffer loss? Ever slowly lose control of something? Ever slowly lose control of everything? Fail? Ever fucking really badly fail?

SCENE 3

WOMAN: This is sort of a juncture, for us. Would getting one of those books of children's names be a good idea?

MAN: Theoretically.

WOMAN: You have to have some feelings. Name some names.

MAN: Lawyer Malloy. Bodhisattva. Steve Stevenson, I don't know. I think Alexander Graham Bell has a certain ring to it.

WOMAN: A first name is fine. And what if she's a girl?

MAN: Then you can name her "You," after you. Or, I don't know. "Simone"? Isn't there a human name "Simone"?

WOMAN: Please, darling, try.

MAN: All right, darling, I will.

WOMAN: Now, think.

MAN: I'm thinking. *(Brief pause)* I've thought. *(Brief pause)* I should speak. This might hurt. What if there's someone else?

WOMAN: There's everyone else.

MAN: No, no there isn't. What if I don't care about this, because I'm in love with someone else. That would be quite a turn. The famous "another woman." What if. She studied trumpet and she's teaching me the harmonica. We play in the snow. I gave her the children's book you gave me that I said I'd lost.

WOMAN: I'm sorry? I'm preoccupied. With the baby, yours, inside of me. You said something about a trumpet?

MAN: I said something about my lying and cheating and going back on my word. Listen to this, the following words: my feelings changed. From away from ones of love.

WOMAN: Stop it.

MAN: I already did. It'll be as if I never started. I would have told you sooner, but, I don't know.

WOMAN: You're serious.

MAN: Not really. I don't know. I am.

WOMAN: What is her name?

MAN: Again, with names. You wouldn't believe me if I told you.

WOMAN: Why not?

MAN: Because I'd be lying.

PROLOGUE: Ah, love.

WOMAN *(Pause)*: How could you do this?

MAN: This? Is that how you would denote my million million feelings: "this"? Or do I mean "connote"?

WOMAN: Just the other day we were talking—

MAN *(Interrupting)*: I know I keep interrupting, but, "The Other Day and The Other Day and The Other Day. Life is but a bucket boy drumming for loose change, a person playing pots and pans on the street as a way to get some food. Or, not really, not at all. That isn't at all what life was, The Other Day, The Other Day, The Other Day." It ends a little weakly, kind of tails off, but how's that for a little soliloquy?

WOMAN: Please listen. Just to this one little thing. I want you to listen. When I was little, before school or anything— *(Brief pause)* You gave her the book I brought back from England? I walked forever. I went through miles of stupid English rain to buy that stupid book. I loved that stupid book. *Sleepy Time Rhymes.* We colored it together. And you gave it away to some bitch to remain unnamed?

MAN: Don't be vulgar. But, that book, I believe you mentioned that book, *Sleepy Time Rhymes.* It made her happy. She loved it, too. She cried over it. We read it to each other and went through it with Wite-Out and uncolored it together. It was our best night.

WOMAN: What did I do?

MAN: Nothing. Somewhere, though, someone did something. It would seem. Once, there was a pretty pretty girl. Maybe she's the one who did something. Time will take care of her.

We'll see what pretty bones her face is made up of. Her, I loved. Unlike you and the woman I'm now leaving you for. Her name is Jennifer, too.

WOMAN: My name's not Jennifer.

MAN: No, I know. I just meant that she's another person with that name.

PROLOGUE: Welcome to a play whose— Parlez-vous anglais? Sprechen Sie Englisch? Niwappi inglappa? Schönes totes Kind, estos zapatos son cuyos? Esti palid. Mimi niliyeona nasema hivi. Wo ist der Zoo? I speak English. Or, I used to. Let us now rejoin— This doesn't cohere. I can't make this make sense. *(He exits)*

EPILOGUE: He just said, "Welcome to a play whose— Do you speak English? Do you speak English? Do you speak English? Beautiful dead child, whose shoes are those? You are pale. I who saw say thus. Where is the zoo? I speak English. Or, I used to. Let us now rejoin— This doesn't cohere. I can't make this make sense." I quote. For what it's worth. Which is probably very little. But maybe not. I'm not big on assigning values. But, it's entertaining to see people in pain, yes? *(He looks to where Prologue has just exited)* We now rejoin the man and the woman. It doesn't matter where.

SCENE 4

WOMAN: You can stop loving me overnight?

MAN: I started loving you overnight.

WOMAN: We took walks. We undressed each other. You said such beautiful true-sounding things.

MAN: Get lost. *(He returns to reading the dictionary)* "Should. Verb. Past tense. Used to express duty, obligation, necessity." *(He has mistakenly read "used to" as meaning "formerly did" rather than "employed to")* What? Oh, *used* to, I see. *(Pause. The Doctor enters. To the Doctor)* What do you think are some good baby names?

DOCTOR: Did you both forget? Everyone's going out on the hill for a big photograph. We're losing daylight, so rush. We need everyone. I would come back if I could. I heard you fighting.

MAN: Just she was fighting.

DOCTOR: One person can't fight.

WOMAN: Yes one can. I was, just. Me, alone, fighting.

DOCTOR: I'm wrong again, then—malpractice, my old friend. But let's go outside. We never get good weather, so let's not let it blow over. Winter is going to kill everything and we want to have a photograph to look at to keep us warm while we suffer through it. I know this is a bad time, but it's for the Crossroads brochure.

(The Woman, Man and Doctor exit.)

PROLOGUE *(Enters, slightly disheveled. He has a glass of water)*: I apologize for the awful languages that I was using before. It's just that ... I don't know. Sometimes we don't ... *(Pause. He regains some composure, resigns himself to continue on)* Anyway. They all go. They stare at the camera. Like life, it's over, like that. Long complicated life histories, over, click. Where did all the talk about the ocean go? Down some drain, out to sea? And you? I wonder how you are. Think of yourself when you were younger. Did you ever love anybody? I'm sure you did. You looked so proud. Your nice shoes and clothes are still somewhere. Maybe you're thinking of that. As you live on, as you lose some more of the rest of your life, quietly, in the dark. I don't know. *(Pause)* Everybody leaves. The photographer gets in his car. Day is over again.

39

EPILOGUE: Right. Right. One more thing. There's more snow in the forecast, moving in like an angry animal from somewhere out over the ocean. If you'll forgive me the simile. Which you probably don't. So I take it back. It's black, out. The freezing shitty night settles. And people do to people what people have always done to people. No big deal. I don't care about the time or where anyone is.

SCENE 5

The Woman, Man and Doctor enter. A long pause. They stand, not knowing exactly where they should be.

NURSE *(Enters)*: Good morning, everyone. *(Pause)* I see our scene has moved to the group therapy room, for group therapy. *(They all move across the stage and seat themselves)* Did someone get sick in the hallway?

WOMAN: Is this an experience experienced by anyone? Where it's just you and someone, and you lay and lie and lie in a room. This someone is lying next to you in the breathing dark but he doesn't know who he is, and that makes you start to slip. And you make the statement: "I am not in control of my body or my mind." And you state the question: "So then what is the 'I' that is the subject of the assertion?" And then you tender the inquisition: "Who is the liar, the breather, the nobody, lying next to me? And who is the one lying inside me, kicking?" You won't recall this time in your life with any warmth. And you feel sick. And as you suffer all that and grow great with mistakes, you can't even count on anyone to be—not even faithful—but just humane? Just at least recognizable? Anyone? Any goddamn body? I never swear.

40

DOCTOR: Why doesn't everybody take a few deep breaths and—
WOMAN *(Interrupting)*: Why doesn't everybody not do that. I've breathed deeply enough, thank you. I think I'll go be sick again. That would be the most expressive thing I could do. Words. *(She gets up, seeming lightheaded)* Excuse me. I'm sorry. I'll be all right. Or I'm wrong. I'm sorry and I won't be all right. And I'm not sorry.

(She walks downstage, stares at the audience for a moment. Perhaps she is thinking and feeling, "It is your need for plays that is causing all this to happen, that is causing me all this pain. Are you happy now?" Then she exits.)

DOCTOR: Why don't I go see if I can say anything. *(He exits)*
NURSE *(Long pause. Not unkindly)*: Well. You seem to be living with yourself. I don't know exactly what to say. *(Pause)* It's supposed to be a beautiful sunset, tomorrow night. Or the night after. Or that's what they said. Why don't we . . . I should . . .

(The Nurse exits. The Man exits.)

PROLOGUE: Traffic lights are changing, clicking, alone across the suburbs, the tundras, the empty urban intersections. I'm picturing this and telling you this. I don't know why. Maybe to help. Maybe I'm trying to help.
EPILOGUE: Click-clack. Tick-tock. This last night is now weeks ago. A new routine has set in. We are in evening. The action moves to a waiting room. Enjoy.

SCENE 6

Lights up. The Woman is sitting, staring into the audience. Pause. Lights down.

EPILOGUE: And to a laundry room.

SCENE 7

Lights up. The Man is sitting, staring into the audience. Pause. Lights down.

EPILOGUE: And to an office.

SCENE 8

DOCTOR: She says she'll take care of the child. She keeps saying, "Me and the world will carry on." Then she looks at a lamp or a pile of books and says, "Won't we, world?" It makes you want to cry to hear.

NURSE: He says he never did well when people tested his personality. Then he says, "It's just a stage." Then he doesn't say anything. Except, then he says, "Everything will end, happily." The comma makes me worry. I listen and nod and say something I've said before.

DOCTOR: And then there's me. I stand here, idly. An empty white coat, a dry pen in my pocket. My oath is to first do no harm. But I don't do anything, ever. Except this. I stand outside and tilt my head and listen to the traffic and wonder if it's people coming or people going and revel at how it all sounds the same. Is that a promising entrance or heartbreaking exit? Then I go make notes, enter a journal entry on a scrap of paper to be left behind or recycled. Maybe I doodle a little design, heave a heavy—I don't know—sigh. I'm glad you're here. I've told you my hobby. What do you like to do?

NURSE: I'm glad you're here. Everything will quiet down eventually. I'm too busy for hobbies. Except reading and skiing. Landscape painting, quilting, calligraphy, comparative philology and . . . I'm kidding. I thought a little levity might . . . I think I'd like listening to the traffic. *(Pause)* Spring will be pretty, the birds and the bees, and your speaking engagement. Then of course you'll have to decide how you're going to injure and embarrass yourself in the inter-hospital softball game.

(They share a little laugh.)

PROLOGUE: Ah, finally, kindness. Love is deep and real and everywhere. All is well and all will be even better. We can see this all around us, clearly.

EPILOGUE: What a pain. I'm sick of the story. I'm sick of you. Next scene. It's got flowers in it.

SCENE 9

The Woman is asleep in bed. The Nurse enters with flowers.

NURSE: Here are some flowers, dear.

WOMAN *(She is waking)*: Was I . . . What did I . . . I was in a field that went down to this water. Everyone was watching me. I looked nice. Someone wrote YOU'RE COLD on my arm. I wanted to thank everyone for being

NURSE *(Interrupting)*: Hello, darling. Easy, slowly. It was just a dream. I know it's hard. Here are some flowers.

43

WOMAN: Thank you, I need to take a bath.

NURSE: I remember wanting to do the exact same thing. After I underwent this same procedure. I remember I had hopes of snow days and photo albums. I was to remain an unwed non-mother. I'm sorry, darling. Forgive me. I was just harking back.

(The Man appears at the door.)

And who is that young man, so boyishly entering. I'll leave you two alone. Yell, if it gets too lonely. *(She exits)*

MAN: They said you were sick.

WOMAN: How kind of them to phrase it that way.

MAN: Is there anything I can get? *(Pause)* Is it contagious?

WOMAN: No. I had them evacuate the fetal material attached to my uterine wall. Can you think up a better name for that? A girl's name? There are so many pretty ones. *(She closes her eyes)*

(The Doctor and Nurse enter. The Prologue leaves his narrator's position to join them. The Nurse is holding a sweater. The Doctor has a tray of food. The Prologue has a heart-shaped box of candy. One by one, they set these things down, on a table or at the foot of the bed, and exit. The Prologue returns downstage to where he narrates.)

(She opens her eyes) That was nice of everyone. You know, it physically hurt. It still really physically does. You don't know. Once, sweat from you got in my eye. It physically burned and I liked it. Will this be going into your play? And do you wonder whether you'll allow me to recover? What would be your name for this? This procedure, you and I, our life? I should go. But I don't think I can walk. So, you. Come on, go. Consider yourself forgiven, your almost pretty

eyes forgotten. Hand me that candy, please. I will be polite up to the end. I was never a person who swore, even though you had me swearing. Please go. No, wait. *(Pause)* Now go.

(The Man exits.)

PROLOGUE: I— I wish— Now we— The— *(Pause)* I could misquote the old books. That might be meaningful. What flowers could grow out of this rocky garbage? A gross of broken statues and a pile of overdue books. Maybe the thunder will say something motherly. Maybe someone will say something kind.

(The Epilogue steps a step forward, pauses, a tiny shrug. He lowers his head, slightly, and steps back.)

(Pause. He holds up a photograph) Here's the picture from the hill that everyone stood on. You can see their breath. Aren't pictures of people beautiful? *(Brief pause)* But, our story! Our scene moves up the coast, to the dazzling, cold, and pacific Atlantic Ocean! Quickly! To a young family, in the sun, happily. With all speed, fly!

(The scene does not change. It is the Woman in bed, still.)

EPILOGUE: Oops.

SCENE 10

WOMAN *(Taking sleeping pills, one with each sentence or so)*: This little piggy went to market. This little piggy is not careful. This little piggy's bladder relaxes, as she wets herself, as she did when she was little. And someone blew my house down. Mein Schönes totes Kind. I will huff and puff and die. *Uff-hay* and *uff-pay*, in Pig Latin. *Ipso facto*, in regular non–Pig Latin. I am killing my body, in English. I'll be fine, don't worry. Dad? Tell me the story of me. A sleepy time rhyme. Italicize my life. This little. *(She closes her eyes)*

(The Prologue stares at the scene of the Woman in bed. He turns to the audience, pauses. He begins to open his mouth, closes it.)

EPILOGUE *(Gently)*: Stop crying. Practice holding and kissing your pillow, for when the day comes you really need to hold and kiss it. This is what I tell myself, softly. There's a philosophy for you. Or, for me. And don't get sick in Europe. Life is a word game. I don't know what else. *(Pause)* Everything is worse, including our desire for improvement. Of a life, a life story, a play. All are awful, worse, the same, but, in the end, to be lived with. Life is fine. It's spring. In fatigue and a lack of creativity, we fall back on the device of a telephone.

SCENE 11

DOCTOR *(Speaking on the telephone)*: I would like you to come down. I need to speak with you about your daughter. *(Pause)* I would like to speak to you in person. Here. *(Pause)* Please come. I'm sorry for being difficult. Thank you. *(Pause)* I really need to speak with you, here. Person-to-person is best. Yes, a right turn after the big wooden ice-cream cone. Thank you. *(He hangs up the telephone)*

(Pause. The Epilogue looks over at the Prologue, who stares into the audience.)

EPILOGUE: Nothing to say? Cat got your tongue, and the rest of your body? No more scribbly poetry to throw at the moment? Lost your nerve? Can't do it? The image gone, disintegrated into synonyms? I guess I understand. I guess I remember, too. *(To audience)* It's weeks later, again. Spring, more flowers. A desk. Sunlight. A patient sits near the desk with his belongings in a bag marked PATIENT'S BELONGINGS.

SCENE 12

NURSE *(Filling out paperwork. The Man is watching)*: Isn't it amazing how I can write upside down like this? Remember that? We're going to miss you around here. Do you have a forwarding address?

MAN: I do, but I don't know it yet. Is the doctor coming in, today?

NURSE: He said he'd try. Do you have any nice plans?

MAN: I'm so sorry. One minute, I was so sure, I completely felt as if I—

EPILOGUE *(Interrupting. He does not believe that the Man should be given the chance to explain himself or apologize)*: Outside—

MAN *(Interrupting)*: I felt as if I—

EPILOGUE *(Interrupting)*: Outside—

MAN *(Interrupting)*: I wish that I—

EPILOGUE *(Interrupting)*: Outside . . . it's afternoon. Clouds, sun, whatever you like. A pretty May day, too late for excuses. Carry on.

NURSE: Did you want to say something, dear?

MAN: Should I say that I was . . . I don't know. What should I say? I never knew.

NURSE: Yes, dear, of course you didn't. I know. *(Pause)* If you get out to Concord, say hello for me. Get down to that wonderful bridge they have. I went there once with a beau. We had quite a time of it down in the weeds by the water. It's one of life's wonders how pretty it is. The river going by, people going by us, us saying to each other, "Quiet. Quiet," while our lives and those people went quietly by. Oh, the daffodils, and all the other flowers, all so prettily named.

MAN: I'll try to go.

(The Doctor enters walking with a cane. His face is swollen. He has trouble speaking.)

NURSE: Well if it isn't you.

DOCTOR: Yub. It ith. *(Trying to say: "Yup. It is.")*

NURSE: How are we today, Doctor Oh-So-Wonderfully-Handsome?

DOCTOR: Nod bad, thang you. *("Not bad, thank you.")*

MAN: Doctor, what happened?

DOCTOR: I wath looging for my trhain thet in the attig and I god thtung by beez. I broak my toe drying to ghet away from thehm. Thirdy-five bee thtings in one segond, they thaid. I cand feel one thide. Bud, ind warth my band thide, ainway. *("I was looking for my train set in the attic and I got stung by bees. I broke my toe trying to get away from them. Thirty-five bee stings in one second, they said. I can't feel one side. But, it was my bad side, anyway.")*

NURSE: I'm sorry?

DOCTOR: It wath my bad thide. For dayging pithurth. *("It was my bad side. For taking pictures.")*

NURSE: Thank goodness your good side was twice as good-looking to begin with. Maybe we'll take some pictures this afternoon.

DOCTOR: Thang you. You are nod thow bad yourthelve. Do wee haff thum way of reathing him? *("Thank you. You are not so bad yourself. Do we have some way of reaching him?")*

NURSE: He'll let us know.

DOCTOR *(To the Man)*: You ghan alwaith contag uth, here. *(Pause)* Whad a fath winder. Lod off yhangeh. *("You can always contact us here. What a fast winter. Lots of changes.")*

NURSE: I'm sorry, Doctor?

DOCTOR: Lahdz, ough, yhanghes. *("Lots, of, changes.")*

NURSE *(She doesn't understand)*: Yes.

DOCTOR: Ihthh— *(He has to swallow)* Ith your vhamly gumming? *("Is— Is your family coming?")*

NURSE: We called a taxi. *(To the Man)* Which you should get out front for. And I think we have some new people arriving. May I walk you to your office?

DOCTOR: Thang you. All hride. Bhee goohd. Wheel mith you. *("Thank you. All right. Be good. We'll miss you.")*

MAN: Thank you, Doctor. Good-bye. I loved—I was— Thank you.

(In the following two lines, the Prologue and Epilogue both begin to speak over one another, then the Prologue needs to pause to drink some water.)

PROLOGUE: Later, the doctor is in his office, the nurse—

EPILOGUE: Not that anyone cares, but—

(The Epilogue stops, steps back, in a moment of kindness and deference, to allow the Prologue to speak.)

PROLOGUE *(He clears his throat)*: Later, the doctor is in his office, the nurse in hers. The body of the woman, gone, and the tiny empty swaddling clothes on a shelf in a store, unbought. The body of the man is in a taxi, and then on a train. He sees the reflection of his reflection looking out the tinted window and sees the land and trees fly past. Towns fly by. People. "Whad a fath winder." There is a long long pause, no sound at all. Like the quiet I deprived us of at the start of this. Excuse me. *(He exits)*

EPILOGUE: It's neither not winter nor not summer. So what is it? The body of the man, some man, is in another white room, alive, staring at another white wall. There was never any woman, never any nurse, nor doctor, nor certainly any man. Isn't that sad? There was never any abortion. There was no toy airplane. So what was there?

PROLOGUE *(Enters with flowers)*: The sun is setting, the great sad past in the air, all of your life in the air. Another sunset, another dusk. The doctor and the nurse soldier on. The beauty of the suffering, suffering.

EPILOGUE: Life. Writing. Try again some other year. This was a mess. The wrong words, too late. This is awful. So sorry. So cold.

NURSE: Isn't it a pretty light? Aren't we lucky.

DOCTOR: Yes. It's a very pretty light. We are lucky.

NURSE: Doesn't it look quiet.

PROLOGUE: Thank you for coming. The End. Good night.

EPILOGUE: Thank you for coming. There is no end. Good night.

DOCTOR: It does look quiet.

(The Prologue has his bouquet of flowers, and, in a simple gesture, he turns and raises them, as if about to present them to someone, though he does not know to whom he should give them. The lights fade.)

END OF PLAY

Production Notes

Casting of Narrators

The Prologue: he should differ—if not physically, at least in terms of demeanor—from the Epilogue. In physical terms, perhaps the Prologue is large, and the Epilogue is skinny. More importantly, where the Prologue should tend toward warmth and geniality in his demeanor, the Epilogue should seem colder, more angular, should even have a flair for a seductive kind of cruelty. That said, they are both narrators, after all, and are therefore generally restrained in their manner; whatever feelings they have about the play and its story (and they should have many strong feelings) should be seen more in their suppression than in their expression. We should see them managing (with a couple of exceptions, mainly in the Prologue's case) to overcome the force of their feelings, or to deny those feelings, or to avoid them altogether, though none of this should be played too obviously or strenuously. The general effect, and this is true of most of the characters in *The Flu Season*, should be similar to that of watching a pane of glass slowly break (to use a metaphor). These are very particular notes describing a very particular effect; don't let them be confusing. There is nothing here that is not in Hamlet's speech to the players (Act III, scene 2). The Prologue and Epilogue believe what they are saying, and they care about the audience (though in very different ways). The play has a close relation to each of their identities and histories. Both narrators remain on stage, except where noted. Finally, though the Prologue is not aware of the Epilogue, the latter is aware of the former.

The Epilogue: as described above.

General Notes about Staging

Sets should be simple. Sets should also allow for quick transitions between scenes. (In fact, the play can move along almost seamlessly, with transitions being made while narrators narrate. Though, if done this way, it should be done sensitively and with meaning, and not just for the sake of speed.) *The Flu Season* is very much a play, as each narrator often reminds us; directors and producers should not put too much money or energy into lavish sets in an effort to make believable what can most be made believable by the actors' performances. Also, a certain humility about theater is expressed by the play, and this humility might be undone by particularly ornate or complicated scenery.

General Notes about People and Acting

People are complicated and behave in ironic and self-contradicting ways that can be seen as tragic or comic and, often, as both, simultaneously. We can contradict ourselves, often severely, almost effortlessly. And we live with near-constant anxiety, though almost all of it is buried beneath (and in fact informs) our normal behavior. The same is true for the characters in this play. This does not mean that the complication and irony or anxiety of the characters need to be "played" in any blatant way. On the contrary. The strongest performance, the most human and most forceful, will often be the simplest and most unguarded. Though the language in the play is not necessarily naturalistic, it is, on the other hand, how these characters naturally speak. This is how it comes out of them. Attention should be paid, in rehearsal, to finding a delivery or a way of performance that, on the one hand, serves the heightened nature of the language and the heightened nature of the characters' circumstances; and, on the other hand, serves to create real and believable characters who speak real and believable lines. Running times will vary, but, in general, pauses should be avoided, except where called for.

Finally, the Prologue and Epilogue are narrators, so they speak with some degree of formality and reserve. But it might be that they (particularly the Epilogue) have, in an earlier life, suffered the fate of the Woman. Or suffered the fate of one or more of the other characters in the play. Thus, their relation to the play is real and immediate and based in feelings (such as love or defensiveness, delight or suspicion). It's also important to note that the Man and Woman are not "crazy people," but are simply people trying to live in the world in which they find themselves. And that the Doctor and Nurse are not unkind, are not even necessarily ineffective, but instead are simply people who are trying to help, despite being somewhat distracted by their own private pains.

Another Thought

The Flu Season could be called an experimental play. It uses some complicated strategies. It should not be played or staged, though, in an overly complicated or radically experimental way. All elements should simply be used to tell the story, the whole story, as powerfully and clearly as possible. Proceeding this way should produce, I hope, an effect that is brave and new and moving and meaningful, rather than just "experimental" for the sake of being experimental.

INTERMISSION

Production History

Intermission received its U.S. premiere in June 2006 at New York's Ensemble Studio Theatre's Annual Marathon of One-Act Plays (Curt Dempster, founder/artistic director). The director was Michael Sexton; the set and lighting designer was Maruti Evans, the costume consultant was Amela Baksic, the sound designer was Brian Petway, the sound consultant was Graham Johnson, the literary manager was Jordan Young and the production stage manager was Carol A. Sullivan. The cast was:

MRS. SMITH	Jayne Houdyshell
MR. SMITH	Brian Murray
JILL	Autumn Dornfeld
JACK	JJ Kandel

Dramatis Personae

MRS. SMITH (and Recorded Female Voice), sixties or so
MR. SMITH (and Recorded Male Voice #1), sixties or so
JILL, twenties or so
JACK (and Recorded Male Voice #2), twenties or so

Setting

The play is set in the audience of a play called *The Mayor*. The time is the intermission between Act One and Act Two. At the beginning of the play, we hear the recorded, slightly stagy-sounding voices of the actors in *The Mayor*.

The play begins in very low light. We see the four actors seated onstage, as if in an audience, barely lit. We hear the beeping of a heart monitor machine.

RECORDED MALE VOICE #1: Nothing is happening yet. This is not the moment. It will very gently come. Very natural and gentle, the moment—when it's time. You can hold his hand. His stately hand. I'll tell you when. Gently, he'll just go. We just turn off the machines. There's no plug; that's just an expression. I'm saying "gentle" so much. It will be dignified, dignity, reality, life, gentle. I need you to sign here.

RECORDED FEMALE VOICE: Words fail me, in the face of this. Living life didn't prepare me for this. Studying English didn't prepare me for words failing me, vis-à-vis this. And I didn't imagine signing anything.

RECORDED MALE VOICE #2: He looks so unpeaceful. So uncalm. Just, the quietly rattling thing at the end of the breathing machine. There were so many things he never got to do, so many sarcastic things he never got to say.

RECORDED FEMALE VOICE: He is a good man, your father. I wonder how life will be for us, in our little city, tomorrow. I wonder how it will be for us the day before that.

RECORDED MALE VOICE #2: Meaning today.

RECORDED FEMALE VOICE: Yes.

(Lights up. We see the four people, seated as an audience, facing the real audience, applauding. Recorded applause plays. One or two people hold programs for a play called The Mayor. *The lighting onstage gives the impression of house lights.)*

MR. SMITH *(Pause)*: Well.

MRS. SMITH: "Well."

JACK: Do you want to stay?

JILL: I guess. I wonder what happens next.

MR. SMITH: I think I'll get a drink, or go to the bathroom.

JILL *(To Jack)*: Do you need to get a drink, or go to the bathroom?

JACK: Not right now. Sometimes, though.

JILL: What do you think so far?

JACK: I don't know if the writing is, quite, I don't know. It's sort of boring. Somebody gets old, somebody dies.

MR. SMITH *(He stretches. A little irked by the above remark. Looks at his watch)*: Yes, sir. I believe I'll go to the bathroom, or get a drink. Liquids, in or out.

JACK *(Looking at his program)*: I think it's a little over-written. Or under-written. And I don't necessarily feel for anyone. And he looked so lively and now he's dying? And people don't talk the way they talk.

MR. SMITH: No, true. Interesting point—people don't talk the way they talk. People don't seem the way people seem. I am not

the way I am. There's a subtlety to someone like me, or someone like anyone, that this play doesn't really capture. But, can
I ask you, who ever died that didn't once look lively?

MRS. SMITH: Dear, please. Maybe there'll be some gunplay and
swearing coming up, something to engage your great intel-
ligence. *(To Jill)* My husband is unthinkably intelligent. *(To
Jack)* Hello.

JACK: Hi. *(Looking again at his program)* I guess the next part is
supposed to take place in the future.

MR. SMITH: Is it.

JILL: It's had its moments. Wasn't that a beautiful scene when
the Mayor stepped down.

MR. SMITH: Little towns like that in New England don't have
mayors, they have a Board of Selectmen.

MRS. SMITH: Did the sound of my husband's anger eating him
alive bother either of you two during the first act?

JACK: A little.

JILL: No, of course not.

MR. SMITH: No? Oh, good.

MRS. SMITH: Wasn't that wonderful when the dying Mayor's
wife came out and made that wonderful speech: "I'm afraid
that the social economists have it wrong. It is the head of
state, and not 'the state,' that will gradually wither away."

JILL: You could see in his eyes he wanted to live. Do you think
he dies?

MR. SMITH: In my limited experience, yes, I think he does—
given time.

JACK: What was the meaning of her crying and eating the tissue
paper?

MR. SMITH: The "meaning"? The meaning. What would be the
meaning of her not crying and not eating the tissue paper?

JILL: That reminded me of someone, or some time, I think, a
holiday. *(Pause)* I liked it, though. And that line: "Whither

our Mayor? Oh, gradually, wither, our Mayor away."
I thought I was going to cry.

MR. SMITH: But you didn't?

JILL: No. But I thought I was going to.

MR. SMITH: But you didn't.

JILL: No. I said I didn't.

JACK: I didn't either.

MRS. SMITH *(To Mr. Smith)*: I haven't seen you cry since that older pitcher pitched that perfect baseball game.

MR. SMITH: Twenty-seven batters up, twenty-seven batters down. That would have been the last time you'd seen me, yes. There was something about the idea of perfection that suddenly seemed so huge and saddening. Someone making history, a little person, in the daytime, the humidity, in the middle of an average July. A human being being perfect, in wait for nothing. You only see or read about that a few times in your life, if even. Think of it. The countability. Little life. How many more shaves, or showers? How many more intermissions? The number would scare you to death. *(Brief pause)* And since when did crying become the standard to measure everything by? When I was little, and I was little, I cried if it was cold out, or if the dog lost a tennis ball under the couch. These were not moments of some wild disheveled intensity, or any soul-forming encounter with the Unknown. I cried to cry. I was little. Little children cry. Grown-ups don't, or do, less. Listen, all of civilization was built on the basis of people having learned how not to cry.

MRS. SMITH: I love when anyone starts a sentence by saying, "Listen." What if that were all the person said: "Listen." *(Long pause)* I almost cried during that part about "whither the Mayor," too.

MR. SMITH: Yes, I almost felt something, too. *(Pause)* Here's a cry. Someone at the animal hospital called to say our dog,

our actual dog, had torn a ligament in her actual leg and—
being too old to risk an operation, and her other legs being
too weak for her to stand on if they amputated the bad one—
would probably best be put to sleep. I cried. I cried, completely, I cried recklessly, not stopping for a second to think
of myself as a person who was crying, or to see myself in
the act of crying. Which I'll always do while I'm crying at the
death or funeral of a person. Always. She. This wasn't that.

MRS. SMITH: Dear?

MR. SMITH: The feelings I felt hearing a neighbor say, "She fell.
She was trying to run and she fell." They're not to be shared
or represented—unless they just were. But you won't see a
play about that. Little dog Emily, filled, filled, nothing-but-
filled with nothing-but-love. In all my years in our animal
kingdom—a boy and his puppy, an old man and his animal,
destroyed. When do you get that? You see that, when? So
have your recreational cry at the sadness of the pretend
Mayor's pretend illness, his even-more-pretend assisted
suicide. But, really, what are you crying for? For what faraway little dog in what faraway little heart? Is there something closer by?

MRS. SMITH: Darling, that was beautiful. Wasn't it? I never knew
you had it in you.

MR. SMITH: Had what in me?

MRS. SMITH: Anything, really. But certainly nothing like that.
Which was beautiful.

JILL: Maybe some people need help.

MR. SMITH: Maybe.

JILL: I mean, crying.

MR. SMITH: I know. *(Pause. A more forgiving tone)* Yes, I think
you're right.

JACK *(Pause. He pulls a handful of change out of his pocket)*: Look at
how many quarters I've got. It's like carrying weights around.

JILL: Wow. Free exercise. *(Brief pause)* What happened to the dog?

MRS. SMITH: She died.

MR. SMITH: She didn't die. I had them put a splint on it. Just to see. She whimpered herself to sleep. Her leg got caught in doors and she gently fell downstairs. Her mood was good, though. I thought she'd get better. When they were doing it, finally, the dog up on a stainless steel table, the person there asked for the dog's name and I said, "Emily," and the dog, who could hardly hear, could hardly walk, her ears went up, because she thought I was calling her to go for a walk somewhere. Through her favorite field, past her favorite flowers. I drove her down there. She was happy. Her ears. They injected the beautiful thing with something. She was happy for the attention and thought it was exciting to be up on a table. I think she felt as if she'd done something right. I've seen complicated things in life, but, this, no. To watch her old eyes, watching me, change, and then see her ears go down and her lowered head lower down the last half-inch. Then, my dog is gone. Or, from her perspective, I am. No better, gentler thing ever lived. I'm sorry, darling—but none did. We buried her bowl with her. It said DOG in nice old-style letters on it.

JILL: She's in a better place.

MR. SMITH: Yes, our backyard. Underneath a piece of sheetrock and a few feet of— Yes, a better place.

MRS. SMITH: She was a good dog. She was like a member of the family.

MR. SMITH: No, in fact, she was not like a member of the family. My father was like a member of the family. I'm like a member of the family. She was The Dog. Always there, living better and truer through life than any of us, by at least a factor of seven. She gave us many beautiful people years. *(He is possibly beginning to cry)*

MRS. SMITH: Are you—

MR. SMITH *(Interrupting)*: Yes. Whatever you're asking: Yes, I am.

MRS. SMITH *(Pause)*: The people are very experienced. The cast. They're good.

JILL: I guess you really loved that dog. Emily.

MRS. SMITH *(Pause)*: Well, yes, I guess he did. He never told me how much. I knew you liked to walk with her, but I thought you just liked walking.

JACK *(Pause. Looking at his program)*: One of the actors thanks her dog. *(Reading from the program)* "Everything important happens before and after everything else has happened. We live and are alive only in the moments in between the moments. Waiting for the heart to stop, the light to change, as the vital signs grow trivial, and the Mayor's eyes close. And after. In the still parts, when nothing else is happening except people by themselves, being themselves, by themselves." *(Pause)* "Be sure to join us next summer for another incredible season."

MR. SMITH: Yes. "Incredible."

MRS. SMITH: I suppose it is just a play.

JILL: No, it isn't just a play.

MRS. SMITH: No?

JILL: I don't know. You know what I mean.

MRS. SMITH: I almost couldn't stand it when he collapsed in front of everyone. Someone with nothing. Papers all over the floor.

MR. SMITH: Do they even have bathrooms or refreshments here?

JILL: Or when the Mayor was saying, "Loosen my tie. Do I have a tie? Could somebody loosen something?" What do you think happens?

JACK *(Nodding toward Mr. Smith)*: His kidneys explode and he dies of thirst.

JILL: That's awful. *(To Mr. Smith)* I'm sorry.

MR. SMITH: Not at all. It's the truth. The gifted child is right. Kidneys fail. People die of thirst. But, son, do you have a mother? Do you love anything old? Have you ever lost anything, slowly? And if not, then, what experience are you hoping to see represented here? You are comparing this to what?

JACK: I didn't mean anything. I know things. I've had feelings about a lot. And I have a mother and she's fine.

MR. SMITH: Oh? Look at her next time you see her. Look at her hair. Note your mother's elbows. See what the long march of these unmonumental moments the program refers to can do to a person, after enough time. To anything living. In real life. Things begin to fail that you never even knew were working. The duodenum. Just you wait. You "didn't mean anything."

JACK: I didn't. I'll look at my mother. I'm just saying I don't necessarily—

MR. SMITH *(Interrupting. To Mrs. Smith)*: Did you say you wanted something?

MRS. SMITH: This is very old-fashioned, somehow. All of us sitting here, having all these feelings, all lit up. It's nice. *(To Mr. Smith)* No, thank you, dear.

JILL *(To Mrs. Smith)*: Did you get another dog?

MRS. SMITH: No.

JILL *(To Mr. Smith)*: Do you have children?

MR. SMITH *(Long pause. No response)*: At least it never gets confusing, with too many little subplots. It stays very focused on the Mayor, the play.

JILL: True. Although I'd like to know more about everybody— you know, who everyone is.

MRS. SMITH: Maybe it's intentional that we don't know that much. That the family is just these ghostly people, just things that make shadows, little noises around the house. It seems true, somehow. Realistic.

JACK: I'm sorry. Is everyone really so moved by this? This isn't that serious, is it? They're all caricatures. These are police sketches of people.

MRS. SMITH: As I sit here and think of them, and think of people I know, I would have to say—

MR. SMITH *(Leaning across Mrs. Smith, interrupting her. To Jack)*: Some day you may see something. A person's head in a certain position, or an animal's. Some little movement, a wife gardening in the distance, anything. In line at the bank or in the middle of a play or traffic, you'll be waiting for something and something else will come, something close enough. There it is, before you: the great It, this vision, your happiness. You'll never forget it. You'll regale people with the tale of it, your memory of the tale of it, with misty eyes, with telltale quivering voice. People will listen, their eyes dry, their voices even, and they'll nod. "You old sentimental old nothing," they think. "Fool." But you will not be a fool, should this ever happen to you, which it probably never will, making you a fool after all.

MRS. SMITH *(To Jack)*: I don't want to gang up on you here, sweetheart. But maybe all people are police sketches of people. We're just smudgy drawings, outlines, rough guides. Height and weight and eye color. I know I am. For instance, *(She stands, a statuesque pose)* what is my reality? I am what?

JACK: Wait, give me a minute. I actually think I'm sort of good at this. Okay, you're an older—

MRS. SMITH *(Interrupting. She sits)*: I was being sort of rhetorical. I was trying to . . . *(To Jill)* Do you get to the theater often?

JILL: Sometimes. More and more.

MRS. SMITH (*Pause. She stands again. She straightens her dress*): My reality is I'm not what I used to be. My reality is trips to doctors, dentists, ophthalmologists, pharmacists and skin cancer specialists, to keep myself from falling apart in my reality, which, as I mentioned before, consists of nothing but trips to doctors and the hospital, to keep me from— My reality is I am dry everywhere. Who I am is the little old lady you will see in the background of things, outliving husbands, walking with serious and grave intent down meaningless streets to save five cents on nothing, with a flower embroidered into one of the three sweaters I wear to fight off the cold of a warm and sunny day. (*She sits next to Jill*) I'm sorry. You were going to say something.

MR. SMITH: Darling.

MRS. SMITH (*Amiably*): "Darling," nothing—darling. You've always had a wonderful knack for reality. No need for any darling theatricality, now. Life is very simple, the next little bit of future. We sit, we watch, we think, we cheer for the actors who played the family, for the actor who played the doctor. We stand, we stretch, check under our seats and go. Underneath all this, something else. And then into the night we go. As with all good and bad things. I've been thinking of the little dog, and how he wrapped her in a shower curtain before he buried her. I've been thinking of the poor little family the dog is survived by. People whose only progress is getting slightly better at not knowing what to do. (*To Jack*) Do you feel for me, necessarily? People talk the way they talk.

JACK: I'm kind of speechless. (*Pause*) I didn't think—

MR. SMITH (*Interrupting. Gently*): Just stay kind of speechless, son. We understand.

MRS. SMITH (*To Jill*): I'm sorry, I know I just asked you—do you get to the theater very often?

JILL: I've been coming a lot recently.

MRS. SMITH: Do you enjoy yourself?

JILL: I do. A lot. Afterwards, I never know what to say.

(The lights dim three times, signaling that the intermission is over.)

JACK *(Pause. Reading from his program)*: "Time: later. Place: a graveyard."

(The lights fade to their initial low setting.)

MRS. SMITH: It's a beautiful experience.

MR. SMITH: Isn't it.

(The lights fade.)

END OF PLAY

TRAGEDY

A TRAGEDY

Production History

A reading of *Tragedy: a tragedy* was held in June 2000 at the Royal National Theatre Studio in London. The play received its world premiere in April 2001 by the Gate Theatre in London. The director was Paul Miller, the designer was Simon Daw, the costume designer was Soutra Gilmour, the lighting designer was Sarah Gilmartin, and the sound designer/composer was Dominic Shovelton. The cast was:

JOHN IN THE FIELD	Tim Flavin
FRANK IN THE STUDIO	Vincent Marzello
CONSTANCE AT THE HOME	Joanne McQuinn
MICHAEL, LEGAL ADVISOR	Roderick Smith
THE WITNESS	George Innes
THE TECHNICIAN	Chris Jamba

Tragedy: a tragedy received its U.S. premiere in March 2008 at Berkeley Repertory Theatre (Tony Taccone, artistic director; Susan Medak, managing director). The director was Les Waters; the scenic designer was Antje Ellermann, the costume designer was Meg Neville, the lighting designer was Matt Frey, the sound designer was Cliff Caruthers and the stage manager was Michael Suenkel. The cast was:

JOHN IN THE FIELD	Thomas Jay Ryan
FRANK IN THE STUDIO	David Cromwell
CONSTANCE AT THE HOME	Marguerite Stimpson
MICHAEL, LEGAL ADVISOR	Max Gordon Moore
THE WITNESS	Danny Wolohan

Something is on the television, relentlessly. A plane crash, probably. Evening dresses and travel guides washing up on a beach out-of-season. Or, it is one of those new little wars. A scene of an empty street where something important recently happened, a scene of people burning certain flags, waving certain others, or throwing rocks and sticks at a space-age military. Before it all, whatever it is, stands a dashing reporter, talking. Perfectly groomed, dressed in appropriate clothing, properly grave as the moment demands. His teeth are amazing. He shouldn't be there. (Maybe he should be throwing a rock or burning some country's flag. Maybe he could cry. Or help sift through the money and underwear coming in with the tide.) The words flow out of him in local time, keeping time with the urgency or melancholy behind him. Real life on Earth, on television. The reporter stands and waits. Then he speaks again. He stands for us, somehow, standing there. He stands for us standing here wondering what we're standing here for. Us, in the wrong place, the wrong time, in a sort of rapture, with life behind us. Us, with only the early technology of our vocabulary, a tongue, trying to identify the rapturous, trying to sum up the miraculous, standing right in front of it. Possibly.

Will Eno
London, April 2001

Dramatis Personae

JOHN IN THE FIELD	handsome, athletic, thirties or so
FRANK IN THE STUDIO	solid, dignified, late fifties or so
CONSTANCE AT THE HOME	attractive, somewhat delicate, thirties or so
MICHAEL, LEGAL ADVISOR	intellectual type, thirties or so
THE WITNESS	male, everyman type, thirties or so

Setting

The setting is a live television broadcast. Each character is at the place described in his name, except Michael, who is at various locations, and will enter and exit the stage. The Witness will periodically appear with John in the Field. Frank in the Studio sits upstage center. Each speaks as if toward a camera. Constance at the Home, where noted, will turn to address a second camera.

Wardrobe

Frank in the Studio might wear a blue suit, white shirt and red tie. John in the Field, more casual clothes, a windbreaker, a sport shirt. Constance at the Home, a skirt-and-jacket suit. Michael,

Legal Advisor, a white shirt and tie, and perhaps at times a London Fog–style raincoat. The Witness is dressed plainly. All, save the Witness, wear small single earphones.

ADDITIONAL NOTES

When in doubt, with respect to certain aspects of staging, it may be helpful to refer to a news telecast. Which is not to say that this play is meant primarily as a comment on the news media. It is not.

The play may begin with a spotlight coming up on John in the Field as he begins to speak, and then lights coming up on the other characters, when they make their initial utterance.

It went down.

—Anonymous

We tried everything.

—Anonymous

It is night.

JOHN IN THE FIELD (*Listening intently*): Now? (*Pause*) Now? (*Pause*) Okay, anytime. (*He relaxes momentarily, then abruptly assumes a reportorial stance and begins speaking*) It's the worst world in the world here tonight, Frank. People are all over, everywhere. Or, they were. Some, hopelessly involved with the grief here at the scene. Still others, passersby to the suffering, slowly passing by, looking, feeling, hoping and believing that they might learn something from these dark times, that they might find some clue about living, hidden in the dusk of the faces of those who have seen so much so fast, and such sadness.

FRANK IN THE STUDIO: The sense of tragedy must be almost palpable there.

JOHN IN THE FIELD: I'm sorry? (*He checks his earphone*)

FRANK IN THE STUDIO: Is the sense of tragedy palpable?

JOHN IN THE FIELD: Absolutely, Frank. You can feel it. One man came by a moment ago, and then, I felt, could not go on. We did all we could to keep him and his hope up until, after a time, his sister arrived, who had seen him wandering on her television, in the background behind me, in her living room at home. When she came and saw him here, she said, "There you are." He smiled. So that was one touching moment in an evening which has been largely bereft of the nice touches normally associated with the soft nights of this season.

CONSTANCE AT THE HOME: I'm here at the home—what? Oh.

JOHN IN THE FIELD: Another thing I should say is, just, what an incredible job the animals have been doing out here tonight. They've just been a delight to watch. You can perhaps see in my background the dogs going back and forth. They've been barking at the dark and generally doing those comforting things they can usually be counted on to do: licking your hand, yawning, circling before lying down, and making their tags and collars jingle. Just regular dog things. This, of course, all, as the hours grow more and more late out here, and we, it seems, learn less and less. Frank?

FRANK IN THE STUDIO: Thanks, John. Well, we'll be tossing and turning with you, staying right here on top of things, trying to get to the bottom of all this, to find some lesson learned in what has been, so far, a startling unsettling night. Constance? Can you hear me? Constance? Are you there? Well, while we're waiting, perhaps it might make some sense for us—

CONSTANCE AT THE HOME (*Interrupting*): Yes, Frank. I'm here at the home of a family we believe may have fallen victim somehow to the event of night, down here, tonight. The scene is quiet. The lights at this simple one-story home are all off. A sprinkler, on a timer, waters the lawn in long, even sprinklings of water. The scene is dark. In the darkness, a floodlight, activated by a motion detector, will periodically flood the lawn and drive with light. What is felt most here is the mystery. The unspectacular mystery. What remains for us to feel—after having knelt down to feel the worn-out welcome mat, after having looked up at the humble shape of a simple house—is, again, the mystery. The feeling that there are deep deep things in the world: house, people, departure, vacancy, to name only a few. *(She turns a quarter turn)* We just a moment ago learned that it was only so long ago that the residents of this modest off-white home gathered on the perfect lawn here, to throw horseshoes and eat food. Also, later that same day, they made a human pyramid. Which, still a little later, in laughter, collapsed. Frank?

FRANK IN THE STUDIO: Thank you, Constance. John?

MICHAEL, LEGAL ADVISOR: It's Michael here, Frank, from the steps of the capitol building. I've just gotten word that we don't know anything more, yet. We are waiting for a disclosure of some sort from someone with, we hope, a clearer understanding of the night, and of the question of liability. We await the comfort of some official language, a smoothly delivered speech from a suntanned man with an easy style and a stunning gold watch. Whereupon, we might be better able to judge whether any of this was justified, and moreover, whether any of this—should it ever end—will ever happen again. And, at the risk of restating the obvious—

JOHN IN THE FIELD *(Interrupting)*: I'm sorry, Michael, John here. Frank, I'm standing next to a man here who happened to be standing right near or somewhere around the horizon as night fell tonight at nightfall. *(He turns to question the Witness, using a microphone, pausing slightly between each question)* Sir, I'm sure you're thinking of home or family or somewhere else or anything, but just let me ask you, did you see any sign to foreshadow the coming dark, anything to indicate that tonight might be unlike any other in the long and star-spangled history of night? Some omen? The famous branch against the window or some infamous wild animal howl? Did anything at all strike you, were you struck by anything striking, anything . . . *(He searches for another word and does not find it)* striking, as you made your way home from work today, as the world was turning away from the sun, and night was starting to fall—or, descend? A piercing scream, a change in the air, a lack of change? Did you sense any signs like that?

THE WITNESS: No. *(He pauses and John begins to move the microphone away from him, and then moves it again toward him)* None.

JOHN IN THE FIELD: Frank?

FRANK IN THE STUDIO: Well, certainly, perhaps, one look—if we're looking hard enough—almost says it all. Constance, having just heard from the Witness, can you, from the text of his remarks, and in concert with what you see there, create a relation that might help to make this make more sense to us?

CONSTANCE AT THE HOME *(Pause)*: I'm sorry?

FRANK IN THE STUDIO: A relation.

CONSTANCE AT THE HOME: A relation. *(Pause)*

FRANK IN THE STUDIO: Yes. A relation. Some relativity. Between the—

MICHAEL, LEGAL ADVISOR *(Interrupting)*: I'm sorry, Constance, Frank. Michael here. I've just received a word from the Office of the Governor and though it helps us gain no greater insight into the night, it is, I believe, meant to ease the uneasy nerves of the people of this state. It reads, "Dear Electorate: A shadow has crept across the soil of our good state. Day is gone. It does not, now and perhaps ever, seem to be coming back. But I beg you, stay calm. No matter how harsh or Cimmerian the injury or insult to your person is or may become. Courage, people. Thank you, the Governor." So. A word of consolation, some sentences of hope, at

the very least a paragraph of words, on this, our—so far—
deepest widest night. As we move further past dinner and
bedtime, and the darkness which has fallen stays down.
"Cimmerian," I'm told, refers to a people who were said to
live in perpetual night. *(Slight pause)* This, of course, being
only a myth. Frank?

FRANK IN THE STUDIO: Thank you, Michael. *(Michael exits)*
Michael is the station's legal adviser. He—I understand
Constance is standing nearby. Can you hear—

*(There is static, interference. Constance is speaking, though with-
out sound. The static ends and we suddenly hear her clearly.)*

CONSTANCE AT THE HOME: —the feeling of the feeling that
you've been left behind. In the night, we hear a voice, a
father sitting down to eat, saying grace, or standing at a
door, hat in hand, saying good-bye. We hear children playing, slowly—unsure whether what can't be seen in the dark
will be there again in the morning. A little girl, a favorite
dress. Behind me, again, a nice house—but no one home.
One wonders where the homeowners went, what they
thought, as they did. Had they some idea, some inkling,
that when havoc was wreaked all over everything that—

*(Static. John's mouth is moving. The static ends and John is
clearly audible.)*

JOHN IN THE FIELD: —but once was all smiles and sunshine,
dear and wild. And now? Well, the people here have died
down, as all people finally do. But perhaps you can see in
my background the dogs and animal life. Can what they are
doing be called "enduring," when they would not call it
that, when they don't even know it's what they're doing?

I don't know. I know that I learned to talk, talking to a dog. A shepherd/collie mix. She was put to sleep, lain on a stainless steel table, while all around her a family wept without understanding. It was a night very like tonight, except for the obvious difference. But very much the same. Heartworm, the diagnosis. The prognosis, nothing. So we're asking that if you have any rawhide bones or chewy things, please send them to the station, attention to me, and they'll be distributed in an equitable and fair—

(Static. Michael enters. Michael is speaking, though we can't hear him. Then the static ends and he's audible.)

MICHAEL, LEGAL ADVISOR: —whether that is relevant. I can say that all parties concerned—and this includes almost everyone—should take great heart in the kind and largely civilized manner in which most of us, however little informed, have acted. I am reminded of a favorite uncle. He gave me a dictionary, which I mistook as the long, sad, confusing story of everything. But he taught me many things about many things. For example: we speak to keep at bay the blooded wolf of loneliness. Or for example: while crashing your car, always steer into the direction of the skid. But now theory must be put into practice, and the stacks of books are pushed aside, as we careen heart-first and bookless into the blackening night. My uncle was—well, avuncular is hardly the wrong word. From the Esplanade, which is empty, this is Michael. Frank? *(Pause. Frank is not paying attention. He's removed his earphone, and is putting eyedrops in his eye)* As well, we should be grateful that the weather has been so generally fair, having hindered us not at all, as we seek to make things clear. Frank? *(Pause. Frank, not paying attention, is putting sugar in his coffee)* What remains to be seen in this complete darkness is how it will change us. We will suffer consequence. Whenever something happens, so does something else. Frank? *(Pause. Frank has dropped his pencil and is looking under his desk for it)* Moreover, and let me add to the above, the sky always has stars in it. It just has to be night-time for us to see them. I was in a car crash once. I forgot to do everything everyone always told me to do. I couldn't even get into an accident right. *(Pause)* Frank? *(Frank is staring off)* Is he . . . can someone . . . Hello. Frank?

FRANK IN THE STUDIO *(His attention returns as he replaces his earphone)*: Thank you. For that. Wonderful. I'm sure you're exactly right. Meanwhile, we have a recording which may enlighten the darkness we now inhabit. Let's have a listen. *(The tape plays. Possibly the sound of a light wind blowing, a watery sound, an old waltz, nothing loud or discernible. All listen intently. Frank is looking offstage, up. The tape plays for a minute or so)* So there you heard it. There it was. Experts in these areas will be listening over and over to see if they might hear a sound which had not been hitherto heard, so that they may then attach some meaning to the—this thus far—nameless experience we now experience. An investigation is underway, so that we might put an end and a name to what we in our simplicity designate as: night. Any thoughts, John?

JOHN IN THE FIELD: So few, really, Frank. *(Pause)* I think the recording speaks for itself. *(Pause)* In fact, I don't know, I'm sure it does.

FRANK IN THE STUDIO: Michael?

MICHAEL, LEGAL ADVISOR: Legally, it all seems allowable, admissible. Humanly, though, humanly, I wonder. Maybe what we heard was the sound of the world kind of "creaking" on its axis. Which I'm told—though there's no evidence to support it—it does. Or maybe it was the leftover hum of some ancient long-dead languages. Or just static. Or almost nothing.

FRANK IN THE STUDIO: Interesting.

MICHAEL, LEGAL ADVISOR: Were you ever in a crowd of people and you suddenly had the feeling that somebody was about to get hit, hard? That something slow and violent was about to violently and slowly happen. Or, that feeling, if it's flu season, and you suddenly realize you're about to get sick, but you're not sick yet.

FRANK IN THE STUDIO: Michael, I'm going to throw it over to John. John, is our witness still there? Can we get a response from him?

(The Witness looks puzzled, perhaps a little frightened. John holds the microphone up to him. The Witness does not speak.)

JOHN IN THE FIELD: No, Frank. No we can't.

FRANK IN THE STUDIO: And Constance? Constance, are you—

CONSTANCE AT THE HOME: Yes, Frank, I'm here. *(She has grass stains on her front)* I think the recording was, in parts, quite beautiful. After listening, we—the crew out here and I—we fell down and pounded on the sprinklered earth here. We did this, perhaps, in hopes that it might know our sorrow, that the earthly world of worldly things might feel our suffering, and know our wonderful physical mystical bodies, which rot. Listening left us also with the knowledge that, once you stop to look, everyone has the most beautiful eyes. Behind me here, the people not here, they are somewhere else, they are out. One hopes that they are somewhere together, talking, touching each other's forearms lightly. It's growing late, with the lateness informing everything, except ourselves. While, somehow, the night seems to be getting smarter. And when you listen, the quiet is not technically that quiet. *(Pause. She listens)* See? Frank?

FRANK IN THE STUDIO: Thank you, Constance. I can only imagine. I'm told Michael is standing by with another word, perhaps another word or two of healing from the Office of the Governor. Michael?

CONSTANCE AT THE HOME: I'm sorry, Frank. Just one more thing. We—the crew and I—we just a moment ago saw a bicycle-built-for-two come going by. The two figures pedaling, one wearing a hat, but neither responding to our calls. We shined a light at them, but they kept going. A tandem bicycle at night, in night. There was a bell on it, possibly shiny, and certainly unrung. Thanks, Frank. Frank, also: a light rain started. Go ahead, Michael.

FRANK IN THE STUDIO: Thank you, Constance. I'm sorry, Michael. But we're going now to our national affiliate for an update as to how this situation affects the country as a whole. Following this reflection on the nation-at-large, we will return to our continuing and hopefully, soon-to-be-over, smaller local coverage.

(Everyone immediately relaxes. Constance attends to her makeup, perhaps tries to remove the grass stains. John does some karate, some tai chi. Frank stands and stretches. Michael makes notes. This lasts for about a minute. When Frank begins again, everyone begins to regain his professional stance, although one by one, and not all at once.)

(Abruptly) We're back. Thanks for staying with us. Word has it there is some word from Constance out at the home, there, the house with all its lights out. Constance? Go ahead. What can you tell us? *(He again removes his earphone, to clean it)*

CONSTANCE AT THE HOME *(Speaking to an unseen crew member, not expecting to be on camera)*: Oh God, I know. Good question. Who knows, really. Most of my memories happened in the sun. My first romance was in day camp. But then again, my father came home in the evenings, so I sort of picture that. We'd put on the radio. *(Brief pause)* We hear music better at night, did you know that? Because of from when we used to have to listen for the sound of some animal coming out of the dark to kill us by our little fires. So music sounds better when it's dark. Music. Because we're listening for our murderer. A shaggy animal with a thirst for blood, a hunger for muscle and bone, lurking somewhere in the bushes and notes. *(She removes some lint from her jacket. A pause. She listens. She sings very quietly. The first song, the "Ode to Joy" from Beethoven's Ninth Symphony. The second, an old drinking song)* "Freude, schöner Götterfunken / Tochter aus Elysium / Wir betreten feuertrunken / Himmlische, dein tum-te-dum." *(A pause. Frank replaces his earphone)* "Ninety-nine bottles of beer on the wall, ninety-nine bottles of beer, you take one down—"

FRANK IN THE STUDIO *(Interrupting)*: I'm sorry, Constance?

CONSTANCE AT THE HOME: I'm sorry, Frank.

MICHAEL, LEGAL ADVISOR: It's somehow my fault, Frank. Michael here, Frank, on the steps of Grange Hall, with, perhaps, a message of healing—as you said—from the governor, I'm not sure. It reads, "Comrades. Please don't despair overmuch, though the rays of light are underfew. I, by the way, write all my own speeches. By hand. Anyway, maybe it will only get harder and darker, who's to say? Most likely, no one. We are individuals in this. But we are a species, too, and I believe it is time that we started to act like one—on instinct, in concert, together, as one: a community, a mob, unruly, united, vicious, wild-eyed, together, bloodthirsty, doomed. And if our sun is dead, then so be it, and in darkness we shall reign and prosper, until we freeze to death. Drive-in theaters will thrive, as people picnic in the dark and eat breakfast by candlelight. Picture it. And so maybe this is the deal, this picture, that the sun will just stay down, leaving everything left in the chaos and obscurity that it was all the time originally in. Quit asking why it's so dark, and start remembering how great it was that it ever got light. Believe you me, if we stay stuck in this fucking darkness, you won't see me crying. So I say, let the looting begin. If you're so afraid, why don't you panic? This is the night of your lives. If I had imposed a curfew before, I would lift it now, and let everybody run wild. Run wild across the world, lovely people, naked and wild, of flesh torn and spirit rash. Every night is the dark night of the soul, but only one can be the darkest, and last. Maybe we should bring back holding hands. Or maybe a bonfire is in order. In the meantime, watch where you're walking. Keep in touch. Be sweet to yourselves. I'm a ghost. Yours, the Governor." He writes all his own speeches, Frank. All of them, all true, I believe. All written from real life. From his real life. From ours. And by hand. I believe. Frank?

FRANK IN THE STUDIO: Okay, thanks, Michael. Some words, some moving words—even some swear words—from the governor, clearly shaken by the disaster of night visited upon his fiefdom. Clearly feeling the strain, the agony, the pain of everything, while trying to put his state aright, in some kinder less-harsh light. A man at the brink of everything. Not unlike a lot like all of us. From the beginning, the first thing the first people were afraid of was the dark. Let us not forget that life used to consist of being born, being scared, sleeping on the ground, getting a stick to protect yourself, shaking through the night, catching a cold, and then dying. We have not come so far that we still don't fear the dark. So the governor is quite right in his noble efforts to embolden us, to buck us up. His message: be courageous, picnic amidst the confusion, and, remember. Constance, what are some other things people could do?

CONSTANCE AT THE HOME *(Brief pause)*: Aren't they probably already doing them?

JOHN IN THE FIELD: People should do the usual things, Frank. *(He refers to his papers)* And these include: licking your hand, yawning, circling before lying down, and making— *(He realizes he is looking at the wrong notes)* No, sorry.

MICHAEL, LEGAL ADVISOR: People might consider, as the governor mentioned, holding hands. Or panicking and rioting. Our earliest ancestors sat in circles and stared into the black sky. Occasionally, someone banged a stick against a tree. Not that it did them any good.

FRANK IN THE STUDIO: Thank you, Michael. Constance, you seem to be—

CONSTANCE AT THE HOME *(Interrupting)*: As for any sign of looting, sanctioned there by the governor, no, as yet, nothing here, so far. There is no sign of anything else, either. *(Pause)* A light rain has stopped. It's quiet still, but still not silent. One hears secret signs of a world amidst the general nothing. One feels the muzzled beating of an ancient heart in the otherwise heartless-sounding grind. I'm editorializing. I don't know, Frank. But we did spot a horse. I did. A gray horse. But I guess every horse is black at night. He wanted water, I felt. I tried to hit him with a rock. I don't know why or what I was doing. Maybe it was my . . . due to some ancient long-dead . . . certainly the horsie never . . . I don't know. I hit him in the eye, it sounded like. He ran away. Galloped, I guess you'd say, if you felt that one word over any other would make any difference. Oh, one more thought— *(She stops)*

FRANK IN THE STUDIO *(Pause)*: Constance? *(Constance turns to address her second camera, but does not say anything)* Constance?

CONSTANCE AT THE HOME *(Patiently)*: I heard you the first time, Frank.

FRANK IN THE STUDIO: Well, then shouldn't you have—

MICHAEL, LEGAL ADVISOR *(Interrupting)*: Perhaps she should have, Frank. Frank, it's Michael here, Frank. And it's my feeling, Frank, based on an analysis of the governor's letters, that things are getting serious, and if they were serious before, then they are more so now, and if they were more so before, then, now, Jesus, Frank, it might be safe to say that they're awful. Hopeless, more or less. Más o menos, en Español, for those people tonight who are listening in Spanish. Frank? *(He exits)*

FRANK IN THE STUDIO *(Irked)*: Okay, Michael. Thank you for that opinion. *(Pause)* Many of our listeners are, perhaps, yes, Spanish, tonight. Every night, I suppose. So, buenas noches, to them. *(A brief pause)* Why don't we go now to good old John, who is afield. He covered the race for governor all last year and may have therefore heard more fully the message we all just only partly heard. John? Okay, John. Go ahead. John?

JOHN IN THE FIELD *(He is holding some papers, which he looks at and then looks up from. He speaks slowly)*: In the interim, I, somewhat out of, out of I don't know what—character? Is that possible? But, anyway, I . . . The governor's right, Frank. Everyone's right, whatever everyone means—stuck with saying, as everyone is, only the words they already know. Such as the words, "I'm dizzy." Or the words, "I keep looking for something to look at." Or, "If I closed my eyes,

I know I would get sick." Or, "I'm alone in this body, and it isn't on my side." Or, "I want my mother here more than everything." Or, "But if she were to come, I would ask her to leave." Or, "Frank"? Or, "Interim." *(Pause)* I think I have heartworm. It's always night, but, sometimes, it's day. That makes sense, doesn't it? Maybe you can see in my background, I don't know—my shadow. Out there behind me in the dark are spoons and knives and mirrors, braces, change, everything—all the glittery things of a well-lit civilization. The love of a young mother and father, when they were young and loving. A dog at a door. A good good dog with a comic and lovable name. All this. All the things that need light, out there in the dark. Everywhere you look, you see your life, no longer there. And if it's dark, well, then, then what? Frank?

FRANK IN THE STUDIO *(Pause)*: Okay, John. Yes, well— Certainly— *(Quietly)* That was John in the field. John, out there, somewhere—reckoning. Trying like all of us to find some way of defining the evening we currently find ourselves in now. Or, I suppose I mean "night," and not "evening." And, "are lost in," and not, "find ourselves in." It is difficult to find the right— We thank you for— Let's go now to— Let's . . . *(He looks at the floor. Pause)*

CONSTANCE AT THE HOME: Frank? *(Pause)* Frank?

FRANK IN THE STUDIO *(He looks up)*: Constance?

CONSTANCE AT THE HOME: Yes, Frank. I'm sorry about the singing. I hope John is okay. He will be. I hope. That's the name of a person who's okay: "John." But, Frank, are you okay? Do you need air or anything? Water? Anything, you know, elemental? Because we've, at least, we've all been standing around outside somewhere, and at least the dark we're in is real. You've had to stay at your desk all this time, sitting with yourself in the artificial light. It must be hard.

(John in the Field appears sick.)

FRANK IN THE STUDIO: I'm fine. Not so hard. But thank you, though, for thinking of me. Maybe I should take a little walk. Now that I start to think, I think I might be overworked. Or sick with something. And John's last report didn't do much to lighten or lift my spirit. The air is very— *(Pause)* The light is difficult.

CONSTANCE AT THE HOME: Oh, Frank. Here I am, about to say the wrong thing to say. Maybe it's not the right time or place, but when is it ever, and where? But, sometimes, when you sign off and say good night, it just sounds so sad. Whatever words you say, the sound of your voice says, "Good night. Farewell. Be Well. We're all going to die. Please be nice." And, "Please, I don't want to have to hear any more news until I have to." I look at the lines of ink going into the pocket of your shirt. Your eyes look tired. You wash your shirt from that day, at night, in the clean bright kitchen. This is long after all the news is over, and your back hurts. Then you try sitting different ways, in different chairs. I don't know if you're the crying kind. Then you have a glass of milk. Frank?

FRANK IN THE STUDIO *(He appears moved)*: Thank you, Constance. It's nice to be imagined. Doing anything. Even if it's only laundry. Which, incidentally, I send out. But thank you. *(He pauses, looks at some papers on his desk)* We go to Michael. Michael?

MICHAEL, LEGAL ADVISOR *(Enters)*: Frank, I'm here at the First Congregational Church, Frank, where no one has gathered. First this, briefly, from the governor, *(He reads)* "I am toying with the idea of declaring a state of emergency; although at this late date in my life, I feel it would be a great redundancy." Secondly, Frank, I always pictured you coming home late to your house, home to some thing that you loved more than anything. Maybe music or scratchy records of famous speeches. You sit and listen until almost when the paper is delivered. There are photographs lining the staircase you don't climb. You look at your books. Then you have a glass of milk. Thirdly, Frank, we have, statistically speaking, every reason to expect night to end. But, in another way of speaking, we don't. Either way, statistically speaking, thanks a lot for all the times when, when I first got to the station, you used to always wave me over to sit with you at lunch. That was really nice. Thanks, Frank. Also, again, it's dark out tonight. It's hard seeing. Frank? *(He exits)*

FRANK IN THE STUDIO: Thank you, Michael. And you're welcome. *(He is regaining his composure)* Well. A night, increasingly and ultimately, of gratitude, as we all stare straightly into the face of that thing which has been staring out at us, all this time. There's a certain—

JOHN IN THE FIELD *(Interrupting. Anxious)*: Frank! I'm sorry! *(Apologetic)* I'm sorry, Frank.

FRANK IN THE STUDIO: Yes, John? What is it?

JOHN IN THE FIELD: Nothing, Frank.

FRANK IN THE STUDIO: It seemed like something.

JOHN IN THE FIELD: I know, it did, didn't it? I don't know. Go ahead.

FRANK IN THE STUDIO: There's certainly a very definite—

JOHN IN THE FIELD *(Interrupting)*: Frank! Jesus. I'm sorry, again. It's this, again. It's physical. I'm sorry, Frank. John, here. I feel sick and weak, and sick. It's my heart. *(He whispers)* My fucking cunt heart. *(Regular voice)* I keep hearing it. I forget to breathe while I listen and there's nothing to look at to stop me from listening. Systole, diastole, systole. The same old story. And I can't breathe. I feel like I can't.

John, here. There's some owl or something out there. Some sound that sounds like that recording. But there's no star, there's no manger, no blazing charioteer. I don't mean to get religious, but what am I supposed to do? I feel so faint. It's dark. My legs are shaky. Am I faint? Frank? *(He is hyperventilating)* It's dark out. Perhaps you can see— I don't know. Sorry. Can what we are doing be called— What do I say, Frank? Please say something helpful.

FRANK IN THE STUDIO *(He doesn't know how to help)*: It's okay, John. John, it's all right. Just—it's okay, John.

CONSTANCE AT THE HOME: Frank, if I could?

FRANK IN THE STUDIO: Please, Constance. Of course you can. Yes, you go ahead.

CONSTANCE AT THE HOME: Thank you, Frank. Breathing is the first thing, John. Just be yourself, which is John, and breathe. Belly rises, belly falls. Think of other people breathing, whole countries, up and down. *(Pause)* Moments ago, John, a car came by. There was a dog with his head out the window, loving life. I know you like dogs. We heard the radio go past, a country song, and then it faded away, the breathing family inside. I don't know if I'm helping, but, darkness is always coming, from somewhere, for somebody.

JOHN IN THE FIELD *(Nodding)*: That's probably true. That's probably true.

CONSTANCE AT THE HOME: The wee hours are always coming, and this is our life, and the race is on. No one yelled, "Ready, Set, Go." Or, "Lights, Places, Action!" No one yelled anything. To think of the world turning and turning and us trying to hold on. No wonder you're dizzy. It's dark inside of us; I mean that as no metaphor. Have yourself looked at by someone. Then look back at them. Don't forget the breathing. Try to envision anything good, John. Frank?

FRANK IN THE STUDIO: Thank you, Const—

JOHN IN THE FIELD *(Interrupting)*: Thanks, Constance.

MICHAEL, LEGAL ADVISOR *(Enters)*: That was nice, Constance. You know, John, sometimes if I'm not feeling well, I lie down. And if that doesn't work, I try to stand up, or sit.

JOHN IN THE FIELD: Thanks, Michael. I'll try that.

FRANK IN THE STUDIO: And also, John, you know, when tough times come, I'll occasionally—apparently—have a glass of milk.

MICHAEL, LEGAL ADVISOR: Right. Excuse me, everyone. A communiqué, from here at the reservoir. I've just been informed that the governor has run away. Here follows the last message he left, before adjourning a meeting in the statehouse and climbing out a window and sliding down a drainpipe: "Good People. It's likely going to be all right. You might be going to be fine. Thank you for your confidence, which I will now betray. You deserved more and better. I looked into myself. I did some soul-searching but didn't find anything. If it makes you feel better, I was going to die anyway. Who did you think I was? What did you think I'd do? Let it go. Bye now, the erstwhile Governor, your former Governor, the Governor." At the bottom, a thumbprint. Half a drawing of an elephant. He's gone. Does this mean he . . . God . . . *(Pause)* He was . . . helpful, I thought. *(He exits)*

FRANK IN THE STUDIO: Yes, he was. History seems to be—I don't know—everything seems to be making history tonight. Dark times call for dark people, dark maneuvers, things that wouldn't make sense on an average sunny Tuesday. And I should think we should feel blessed to be witness to all this. Speaking of the same, how's our witness out there, John?

JOHN IN THE FIELD: Here he is here, Frank.

(John holds his microphone up to the Witness, who looks at it, and then at John.)

THE WITNESS: I have heart— *(Pause. He clears his throat)* I have heart trouble in my family, too. I don't eat any salt.

JOHN IN THE FIELD: Right. Good. *(Pause)* Go light on the salt. Frank?

FRANK IN THE STUDIO: Thanks, John. We might remind everyone to—

CONSTANCE AT THE HOME *(Interrupting)*: I'm sorry, Frank. But this just in. We've discovered a note out here at the house I'm at, or, standing out in front of. Held down by a few pebbles, out back here on the deck, small, white, written in a writing now running with the weight and dew of the night. Whether it's in a woman's hand or a man's hand, we cannot tell, but it is recognizably human handwriting. It reads: "Hey you— How are things? I waited and then I left. Let's try and talk this week. Come over and let's listen to music. I hope I see you soon. Isn't the sky strange? I have to run. Guess who I ran into today? Call me. Sincerely, Me." Plainspoken, and to the point, written in a loopy American calligraphy, lying here amidst the grass slowly growing in the night. Something illuminating should be said.

FRANK IN THE STUDIO *(Pause)*: Constance, any ideas as to who might have written it, and what it might have meant?

CONSTANCE AT THE HOME *(Pause)*: I'm sorry, Frank—I wasn't listening.

FRANK IN THE STUDIO: Don't you have an earphone on?

CONSTANCE AT THE HOME: I do. But I was listening to something else.

FRANK IN THE STUDIO: I thought it was quiet where you were.

CONSTANCE AT THE HOME: It is. But I was thinking.

FRANK IN THE STUDIO *(Pause)*: About what?

WILL ENO

CONSTANCE AT THE HOME: Nothing. I don't know. Myself, and that horse. Everything. My girlhood. What I did with boys. About coming home when there was no one home. And how a certain life kept coming at me, which was mine. And how now I have to live it, as me. Because why? Because of some little thing that I saw when I was little? A glint on some car keys, or a shadow on a wall, to which I mistakenly attached some mistaken little meaning? So now my life lives itself out, in revisions of revisions of something that was blurry to begin with? I wish that note were for me. I quote, "Let's talk this week. Come over, for music." Or whatever it said. That was the greatest thing I've ever read. The gentlest. And, I feel, the most— *(She pauses, stops)*

FRANK IN THE STUDIO *(Pause)*: The writing was, yes, it was wonderfully readable writing. It would make anyone feel good to have been written that. Thank you, Constance. Meanwhile, I'm sorry, we return again now to national coverage for another word on the larger story of the story of our nation in night.

(There is a difference from the earlier break. There is little activity, an air of dull terror. Michael enters. Generally, everyone stares ahead for about a minute. Then Frank returns to the broadcast.)

Apparently, there's trouble with a transmitter somewhere. We'll have something for you soon. Michael, do you suppose—

MICHAEL, LEGAL ADVISOR *(Interrupting)*: This is Michael at the White House, saying, Está Miguel a la Casa Blanca. And, no, I do not suppose. No official word, but we'll keep waiting. Born to wait, wonder, and die, were we. By the way, can you see me okay? Darling? What's that word that means crepuscular? Or is it just "crepuscular"? I'm imagining a woman in my history. I can almost see her in the murk. My love, my life! Let us convene in a dry and golden wheat field, where I, on bended knee, will then proclaim that: *(Reportorial style)* "This is Michael, on bended knee, in a dry and golden wheat field." Frank? *(He whispers/mumbles a few more words. They are indiscernible, though they have the rising intonation of a question)*

FRANK IN THE STUDIO: I think there's been a . . . Michael, what did you say?

MICHAEL, LEGAL ADVISOR: Oh. I don't know, Frank. I don't know. I wish it was nothing. *(Brief pause)* It suddenly strikes me—I should probably have never have been born. Maybe I should follow the example of the governor and of your better Roman emperors.

(The following exchanges move quickly.)

CONSTANCE AT THE HOME: Michael?

FRANK IN THE STUDIO: Jesus.

JOHN IN THE FIELD: John? Wait—John is my name.

MICHAEL, LEGAL ADVISOR: Sir?

FRANK IN THE STUDIO: John. Everyone?

CONSTANCE AT THE HOME: It may be untimely of me to say, but, I just heard a hot-air balloon going by. Floating, overhead, in the dark. That's a curious reaction to things, to go ballooning. Everyone?

MICHAEL, LEGAL ADVISOR: I'm floating overhead, in the dark. In a way. And everything I've ever said was untimely of me to say.

FRANK IN THE STUDIO: People, please.

JOHN IN THE FIELD: Frank, it's night. Also, I think I might be having a stroke. Or something very personal like that. Back to you, Frank. Or should I say, *(Spoken exactly as before)* Back to you, Frank.

FRANK IN THE STUDIO: It is indeed. And we—

MICHAEL, LEGAL ADVISOR *(Interrupting. Sadly, gravely, in his normal reportorial style, without any regional accent)*: The governor, he gone. They ain't no moon no more. Nothing shining anymore from on high to down upon our dull and raggedy procession. *(Brief pause)* I thought I'd try something different.

JOHN IN THE FIELD: This is John, crapping out.

CONSTANCE AT THE HOME: Sorry, has the word dusk been used, yet?

FRANK IN THE STUDIO: Yes, since you ask. I think, once.

CONSTANCE AT THE HOME: I thought, once. Dusk. I just saw something I thought was a person, whirling in the wind. But it was only a person's clothing, hanging on a clothesline, whirling in the wind. A common mistake. Anyone?

FRANK IN THE STUDIO: Maybe it might be best for us to try to hear a little more on the political situation. Maybe we can do that. So, Michael?

MICHAEL, LEGAL ADVISOR: There's no political situation anymore. And I think we've heard enough name-calling for tonight. If I may be frank.

JOHN IN THE FIELD: A person isn't a person's name. I used to not understand this. But I was such a baby when I was born. We had an important dog when I was little. I named it something, some name, and that's what it answered to, its whole life, until it went deaf, or didn't answer anymore, and then died, or, started shivering, and then died. But that's what happens. Jolly was her name. Here, Jolly. Sit, Jolly. Please stop shivering. Don't die, Jolly.

CONSTANCE AT THE HOME: "Jolly." I don't mind mine. It isn't the most popular name in the world: Constance. Frank was very popular at one time. Frank?

FRANK IN THE STUDIO: Yes thank you. Frank is a fairly popular name. But, Michael, I'll try again, any word from the lieutenant governor? Is a swearing-in on the horizon?

MICHAEL, LEGAL ADVISOR *(In exasperation)*: Oh, Frank, Frank, Frank, Frank. *(Reportorially)* Frank? *(He exits)*

FRANK IN THE STUDIO: Okay, Michael, very good. John, please, who would take over for the governor, here?

JOHN IN THE FIELD: Not me. Not any animals, either. For the animals are gone, having scampered off, as all animals finally do. Leaving here, quiet. I wish I had something more to tell you. I don't know. *(Pause)* Can't anyone in this family talk? You know nothing of my life. I'm a sixty-eight-year-old woman. I was quite a looker in my day, but now I stare out a window. My son's name is John. He works for the news. He was born with a murmur. He gets his eyes from his father and me. He reads to our dog. Strange boy. I wonder what will become of him. *(Pause)* Would you listen to me? I'm starting to sound like my mother. What am I starting to look like?

FRANK IN THE STUDIO: All right, John. We're all very—

CONSTANCE AT THE HOME *(Interrupting)*: My father, now dead, is quite a talker. Always a story, some quote. But he's neither here nor there. Nothing is coming riding by. The note is lost or blown away. Likewise, the family here. The sprinklers, off, as strangely as they came on. There's a seashell from some sea lying in the yard here. It doesn't look serious. I—on the other hand—I feel I do. Frank, would you say that you'd say that I was a beautiful and serious woman?

FRANK IN THE STUDIO *(Pause)*: Constance. I—

CONSTANCE AT THE HOME *(Interrupting)*: I thought so.

MICHAEL, LEGAL ADVISOR *(Enters)*: Sorry to interrupt. A confession. They should have never let me use the alphabet. This is a difficult case. But, the defense rests. There is no defense. I've weighed both sides very carefully. I don't care about either one. The fact-finding is over, none having been found. And we all file out saying, "No comment." File out, not even saying, "No comment."

FRANK IN THE STUDIO: Michael? Goddamn it, Michael! John—

JOHN IN THE FIELD *(Interrupting. His face is bloodied)*: The news is no more newsworthy from here, Frank. The apple doesn't fall very far, Frank. I'm forgetting some part of the expression. Do you have any birthmarks, Frank? I once knew someone, she had some. We stopped seeing each other. I hope she's dead. She was American, which is a beautiful word. We met at an animal rescue league. I'm making incredible sense. To rephrase that slightly, I hope she's alive. She is forever—

FRANK IN THE STUDIO *(Interrupting. In his monitor, he sees John's bloody face)*: John, my God. Are you all right? What happened?

JOHN IN THE FIELD *(Touching his hand to his face and then looking at his hand, he realizes his nose is bleeding)*: My nose is bleeding.

FRANK IN THE STUDIO: Can you get a handkerchief or anything to stop the blood?

JOHN IN THE FIELD *(Amiably)*: "Stop the bleeding." That's very good advice. *(Brief pause. Awkwardly)* I'm sorry, I don't know what I was saying before. *(Brief pause. Confidently)* No, wait—I remember. I hope she is alive. She's forever in my heart, which is broken, and has been since birth. Does anyone else miss anyone? Is there a sister from somewhere, coming? Perhaps you can't see, just over my shoulder, anything. And I'm bleeding. And I'm saying, "I'm bleeding." And I'm sick and signing off. Off into the—what would be a beautiful word? "Distance"? *(He tilts his head back to stop the bleeding, looking straight up)* Distance.

CONSTANCE AT THE HOME: I hit a horse with a rock. It's bleeding somewhere, too, looking up, an animal. Nothing else. Except, there's a ceramic rabbit on the lawn out back. A pretty ceramic rabbit, with one ear broken off. Nothing else. Except, a ceramic deer, three legs and a crack in its head. The floodlight that goes on when it senses any motion hasn't gone on for the longest time. All this ceramic wildlife, and, me, the most ceramic of all, here amidst—

FRANK IN THE STUDIO *(Interrupting)*: In our continuing effort to keep you informed, we now go to the Emergency Broadcasting Network. The years of testing are over, the phrase "an actual emergency," now a reality. And, we go, now. *(A problem. Pause. There is no sound, nothing)* Obviously, more technical trouble. Not surprising. We hope to . . . *(Pause)* Constance, are you there? *(To audience)* We'll get you that message as soon as we can. Constance, I know you can hear me. I hear you breathing. *(Pause. Constance is frozen. John's head is tilted upward. Michael looks down)* Anybody? John? People? *(Long pause)* Yes? I'm sorry? *(Brief pause)* If I can keep going, then anyone can. Listen, it's nighttime, so we pray for morning. Should morning come, we pray for afternoon, and then, by then, for night. This is the natural ritual. People! Somebody answer me! Is there a responsive person somewhere? *(Brief pause)* Someone who could tell me a little story? Something about the renaming of a street, or about something funny someone said in school today? Some little words? Now!? Could somebody help me? Could somebody help the person who is speaking right now? Does not one of you realize what it means for me to ask that!? To talk like this? To be, like this?

CONSTANCE AT THE HOME *(Pause)*: I don't know, Frank.

MICHAEL, LEGAL ADVISOR: Yo no sé, señor.

JOHN IN THE FIELD: I know.

FRANK IN THE STUDIO: Yes? John?

JOHN IN THE FIELD *(Brief pause)*: I don't know, Frank.

FRANK IN THE STUDIO: Well. How unknowing of everyone. "In the lawn-mowing tones of speeches unspoke, in a light wholly absent, by a river by a willow, there did the dark horses of the thrashing—" Forget it. I'm sorry, forget it. I don't have the time or breath to misquote old poetry. *(Pause)* Jesus. *(He checks his pulse)* Oh boy. Oh God. I think I'm going to be sick. I think I'm— John, anyone, I feel like I'm— Please, John, tell me what did you do for your heart, before? Did you take something? Is there something— John?

JOHN IN THE FIELD: I was lying, before.

FRANK IN THE STUDIO: You weren't having trouble?

JOHN IN THE FIELD: No, I was. I really was. I was lying, just then.

FRANK IN THE STUDIO *(Deep breaths. Takes some pills. He recovers, somewhat. He regains his equilibrium, though with a difference. The next line is said sharply)*: Thank you, son, for your honesty. Constance, please be daughterly with me. Maybe you could describe your environment, out there. Even, whatever season we're in. You don't have to make sentences. You could give us a list. Just some nouns. Are there daffodils? Or snowbanks? Are there geese, flying in any direction?

CONSTANCE AT THE HOME *(Pause)*: There is some—

FRANK IN THE STUDIO *(Interrupting)*: Yes?

CONSTANCE AT THE HOME: I'm not finished.

FRANK IN THE STUDIO: Of course, I'm sorry. Go ahead.

CONSTANCE AT THE HOME: —fog.

FRANK IN THE STUDIO: What would you say the visibility is? Our visibility must be practically—

CONSTANCE AT THE HOME *(Interrupting)*: Enough. No more, Frank. Please don't speak to me like that anymore. *(Brief pause)* That's all. *(Brief pause)* Except, my father liked horses. Except, I saw one. I'm a terrible person. But, who isn't? No wonder everyone is never home. No wonder it's just the remains, by the time I always get there. *(She turns to her second camera)* I deserve nothing, and I thank you all for giving me it.

FRANK IN THE STUDIO: Constance, I don't think that's true. You—

CONSTANCE AT THE HOME *(Interrupting)*: Spare me your thoughts on what you do not think is true.

MICHAEL, LEGAL ADVISOR: Michael here, Frank.

FRANK IN THE STUDIO: Yes?

(Pause. Michael says and does nothing.)

JOHN IN THE FIELD: A vacuum. Nature hates moments like this.

FRANK IN THE STUDIO: Nature does. Nature insists on—

JOHN IN THE FIELD *(Interrupting)*: When I was six, this was fairly impressive: A, B, C, D, E, F, G—ah, but I'm sure you all know how that turns out. This concludes myself. You?

FRANK IN THE STUDIO: Okay, John, let us—

JOHN IN THE FIELD *(Interrupting)*: No, let us not. Let us be mum, for so are the gods. Hi Mum. I quit. Go to someone else. Roll some video of a family at the beach or a limp flag in the historical sun. There's nothing here. Cut away from me. Go to black. I am.

FRANK IN THE STUDIO *(Brief pause)*: John, what about all your animals? And the lone man who was walking around, with the sister who came in from home? You had such enthusiasm. Don't we have a duty? At least, a curiosity? I know we're all very tired. *(John tilts his head back)*

MICHAEL, LEGAL ADVISOR: Michael, from here on the missteps of my life, Frank. Legally, everybody is going to be dead.

Legally, everybody leaves you. Let us sit in circles on the
ground in the dew and swap stories of dead governors and
dying legal experts. I shouldn't say anything more. I don't
think I read the dictionary closely enough. I don't think
I did anything closely enough. This was Michael.

CONSTANCE AT THE HOME: As for here, there isn't anyone here.
The point is finally driven home, at this empty house. The
grass will yellow, then blacken. The house will rot, the
driveway crumble, the sprinklers freeze. The human pyramid will collapse, still a little later, in laughter. Girls will die,
Frank. *(Pause. She is trying not to cry and is mainly succeed-
ing)* I have something stuck in my eye. And something else
stuck in my throat. And my life is stuck in my body, which
they will stick in the earth. Everywhere I look are signs of
people having left. Was I born to stand outside, talking
about inside? I give up. I can't keep up with all the leaving
people. With the fucking thinking and speaking. I'm sorry.
Frank, I'm sorry for swearing. It won't happen again.
Nothing will. I'm sorry.

FRANK IN THE STUDIO: Constance? John? God. *(Brief pause)*
Constance? *(A long, long pause. Clearly no one else is going to
speak)* When I was younger— Years back, when I used to—
People have sometimes asked—or, to do— *(Pause)* To do this
job was always my dream. To be trusted and turned to and
believed in. For years of weekdays, I grew, and felt myself
growing, to become all those things. Comforting. Trusty.
Someone. But, no, sorry. I didn't anchor anything. I get
older, every weeknight, without change. The flashlight is
dead and we are left darkling—as we used to say in my
youth, which is also gone, with no remains.

THE WITNESS *(A long pause. He steps into John's position, looking
at and around the camera)*: Is all this still on? Hi, Frank? I'm
that witness that John out here interviewed earlier. I've

been standing here listening, *(Motions toward camera)* through the thing on the thing here. Listen, I think you're great at what you do. You spoke at my school. You seem nice. Constance, if you can hear this, I love you, I watch you all the time. John out here is the best. I remember once he covered some storm in a raincoat, live. And Michael, on the steps of all-over, talking about the legality of things. Everyone's so great. We listen for you. I do. The stories and thoughts. I like the news. Frank works so hard. Come on. Everyone's waiting. *(Brief pause)* Is it supposed to rain, later?

FRANK IN THE STUDIO *(Long pause)*: It seems there is no word.

THE WITNESS: I guess not. *(Brief pause)* I could say what I saw, tonight. I'm not seasoned, or eloquent, like John and them. But I was there, I was standing around. This is my custom. It was sort of twilight. A plane went flying by, a plane did, and made a trail across the sky. I stared. Like this. A dog barked at something. Someone was teaching a baby how to walk on the sidewalk. Lights started coming on, with people coming home. And all this stuff, this whole neighborhood of stuff, I saw. I don't ever remember feeling exactly like I felt. I remember little stuff. There were some birds in a tree, finishing up singing. Someone came walking by with a garbage bag. I smelled the ocean, which we live nowhere anywhere near. I thought about an ocean. Bugs banged against the outdoor lights. It felt suddenly really sad, I felt, but also not sad, looking at the street in that light. Then, I heard someone calling somebody's name for them to come in and eat. And then, night fell, like usual. But differently, sort of. *(Pause)* That's all, from what I saw. It would be like that, at the start of the end of the world, I guess, wouldn't it. This is all. I thought it was pretty. What do I know? Except all that.

FRANK IN THE STUDIO: Thank you. Thanks. The night has produced an eloquent man.

THE WITNESS: Well, I don't know. I heard words around the
house, you know? Who knows.

FRANK IN THE STUDIO: Yes. *(Pause. He is nodding off)* I'm listening, I'm sorry. I'm very tired. I'm not well. I . . . *(He whispers)* Jesus, Jesus. Ironic, my awakening in life would happen at night, with me having grown so tired, so sleepy and
sick of it all.

THE WITNESS: I know. *(He doesn't understand the irony)* The
irony. *(Pause)* Frank, once I saw the governor in person. He
was filling his car up with gas. He was wearing shorts and
sunglasses. *(Frank doesn't respond)* True. *(Pause)* How
about—well, no, that's no good. *(Pause)* If I ever asked for
a story at night, either my mother or father always told me
this one. Let's see. Once there was a world and it had, you
know, everything in the world in it. Rocks, trees, oceans,
animals, people, houses, governments. All of it. It was great,
everyone thought and felt. Then everyone started to imagine it getting ruined and run down. And that started happening in reality. People started hurting and killing everyone. But then this boy or girl was born that everyone loved
due to their beauty. And the child said to everyone, "I'd be
scared, too." So everyone was scared together. And all their
worries turned into a sort of comfort. And their doubts
about things turned into a kind of faith, sort of. New people were born during this. And new words were invented
to talk about people with. Newness, like, reigned over the
world in the story. Then a bright white horse showed up.
Then I always fell asleep. *(Frank appears asleep)* At the end,
though, I bet my mother or father whispered, "Sweet
Dreams." *(Brief pause)* I can almost see them, leaning over
and pulling the sheet up and whispering something simple

like that over me in my dark room. "Good night, sweet dreams," someone is whispering over me, because they loved me and it's nighttime and they wanted to try to say something. *(Softly)* Frank? *(Pause)* "Good night, sweet dreams," they whisper, and then walk backwards out the door, and close it.

(The light fades.)

END OF PLAY

Will Eno is author of the hit play *Thom Pain (based on nothing)*, which won many awards at the Edinburgh Festival Fringe before transferring to London and New York. It played for one year Off-Broadway, was a finalist for the 2005 Pulitzer Prize, and went on to be produced throughout the U.S., and in many languages around the world.

In 2007–2008, *Oh, the Humanity and other good intentions,* a collection of short plays, ran at the Flea Theater in New York. His play *Intermission* premiered at New York's Ensemble Studio Theatre's Annual Marathon of One-Act Plays in June 2006 and was published by the *Antioch Review.* In 2003, *The Flu Season* premiered at the Gate Theatre in London and then was produced in New York by the Rude Mechanicals Theatre Company, where it won the 2004 Oppenheimer Award for best debut by an American playwright. *Tragedy: a tragedy* was read first in 2000 at London's Royal National Theatre Studio; it received its world premiere at the Gate Theatre in 2001 and its U.S. premiere at Berkeley Repertory Theatre in 2008. An excerpt of the play appeared in the June 2006 issue of *Harper's* magazine. An excerpt of his new play *Middletown* appeared in the Summer 2007 issue of *The Literary Review.*

Mr. Eno is a Guggenheim Fellow, a Helen Merrill Playwriting Fellow, and a Fellow of the Edward F. Albee Foundation. He also won the first Marian Seldes/Garson Kanin Playwriting Fellowship, for which he was nominated by Edward Albee. In 2006, Mr. Eno served at Princeton University as a playwriting teacher and a Hodder Fellow. During 2007, he served as a Fellow of the Cullman Center of the New York Public Library.

His plays are published by Oberon Books in London, and by Theatre Communications Group and Playscripts, Inc. in the U.S.

Mr. Eno lives in Brooklyn.